WIFE BATTERING:
A SYSTEMS THEORY APPROACH

PERSPECTIVES ON MARRIAGE AND THE FAMILY
Bert N. Adams and Reuben Hill, Editors

WIFE BATTERING: A SYSTEMS THEORY APPROACH
Jean Giles-Sims

In Preparation

CONFLICT MANAGEMENT IN MARRIAGE
Stephen Jorgensen and David Klein

THE BLACK FAMILY
Walter Allen and Richard English

WIFE BATTERING
A Systems Theory Approach

JEAN GILES-SIMS
TEXAS CHRISTIAN UNIVERSITY

FOREWORD BY MURRAY A. STRAUS

THE GUILFORD PRESS
NEW YORK   LONDON

For

John Edward Giles, Gregory Snowden Giles, Andrea Dorothy Sims

© 1983 The Guilford Press
A Division of Guilford Publications, Inc.
200 Park Avenue South, New York, N.Y. 10003

Printed in the United States of America
Second printing, March 1984

LIBRARY OF CONGRESS CATALOGING IN PUBLICATION DATA

Giles-Sims, Jean.
  Wife battering, a systems theory approach.

  (Perspectives on marriage and the family)
  Bibliography: p.
  Includes index.
  1. Wife abuse—United States.   2. System analysis.
I. Title.   II. Series. [DNLM: 1. Spouse abuse.
2. Systems theory. HV 6626 G472W]
HV6626.G54   1983   362.8'3   82-15555
ISBN 0-89862-075-9

Foreword

How can a woman who has been repeatedly assaulted by her partner later marry him? Why does a wife who has experienced serious injuries and whose very life has been threatened by her husband's attacks continue to live with him, and then, after escaping with the help of a shelter for battered women, return for more of the same? How can the men involved commit such atrocities against fellow human beings, and especially against the women they love?

These are some of the issues addressed by Jean Giles-Sims. Her study of 31 women whose relationships with their partners are characterized by these ironies moves us much closer to an understanding of wife beating. It is about time, because wife beating is an age-old phenomenon. No one knows if its frequency has been increasing or decreasing in recent years because there are no accurate statistics for previous historical periods. What we do know is that for a variety of reasons (such as the impact of the women's movement and the national anguish over violence due to the Vietnam war, riots, assassinations, and violent street crime) there has recently been a vast increase in recognition of the problem and a commitment to do something about it. There has also been a vast increase in the volume of scientific study of this formerly ignored aspect of the family.

The Family Violence Research Program at the University of New Hampshire is representative of that trend. The first study was done in 1970 and the first two papers were published in 1971. In the ensuing decade, 27 different members of the program have produced about 100 papers and nine books, of which Jean Giles-Sims's work is the latest. Yet this program has produced only a small part of the large and growing literature on wife beating.

One should not, however, be overly sanguine about the contributions of social scientists to the problem of wife beating, nor overly proud of the scientific quality of the work. There is more quantity than there is quality. The reasons for this include the newness of the subject as a topic of scientific study, the blind spots imposed by implicit and explicit ideological commitments, the depreciation of applied research within social sciences such as sociology, and the inherent difficulty of researching such a sensitive issue. Whatever the reasons, two of the major deficiencies have been a failure to ground the investigation in a sound theoretical framework, and the absence of studies which follow people over time as a means of understanding the social processes that give rise to this puzzling phenomenon. Jean Giles-Sims's work is a welcome exception to both these shortcomings.

Wife Battering: A Systems Theory Approach is, as the title suggests, one of the few empirical studies that uses a clear theoretical framework. It applies "general systems theory" to develop an explanation for what would otherwise be a collection of odd facts about human perversity. Of course, the validity of this theory is not proved in a statistical sense by these 31 cases. Rather, its validity depends on the depth and believability of the case studies that are the core of the book. Fortunately, Giles-Sims's case studies are so vivid that readers can almost reexperience the web of relationships and events which produced the violence. The end result is a genuine step toward explaining the paradoxical combination of love and violence that occurs so often in marriage.

Giles-Sims's work is unique in combining this theoretical grounding with a longitudinal research design. Actually, there are two longitudinal studies. The first is based on a retrospective reconstruction of the events leading up to, and subsequent to, acts of violence experienced by 31 women who sought the assistance of a "shelter" or "safe house" for battered women. The second longitudinal analysis is based on a prospective design. Of the 31 women initially studied, it was possible to reinterview 24 four to six months later. The follow-up study revealed that over half had returned to the same men from whom they had sought refuge. The author's follow-up interviews provide revealing data on violence subsequent to the shelter experience, and on the social processes which produced such a high rate of return. Lest anyone suspect otherwise, it was not usually because these women and their partners had reconstituted their relationships on a new and nonviolent basis!

The combination of general systems theory and empirical data on events in the life histories of 31 women made it possible to construct an analytical model which goes a long way in explaining how wife beating can become a stable pattern of marital interaction. But as Giles-Sims is quick to note, the fact that violence in marriage is explained by the very nature of marriage as a system of social relationships, does not relieve either the participants or the larger society of responsibility for the violence. Rather, her findings concerning the social processes that bring about marital violence suggest what really needs to be done in order to deal with the problem.

Can any more be asked of social research than that it be on an issue of vital importance to individuals and to the society, that it explains why the events occur, and that it suggests what can be done about it? That might seem sufficient. But Giles-Sims's work goes beyond these criteria: It is also readable and understandable. In part this is due to her ability to put things clearly. It is due also to her ability to establish rapport with her subjects so that they could tell their own stories in the depth and intimate detail that readers need to understand the full complexity of the social processes that produce wife beating.

Murray A. Straus
Family Violence Research Program
University of New Hampshire

Preface

In recent years there has been an increased interest among family scholars in the general systems approach to understanding family processes (Gelles & Straus, 1979; Kantor & Lehr, 1975; Hill, 1971; Straus, 1973; Watzlawick, Beavin, & Jackson, 1967). This interest stems from the potential systems theory concepts hold for the analysis of the whole family system, and how members act, react, adapt, and develop stable patterns of interaction over time. Buckley's (1967) application of systems theory to the social sciences provides the basic formulation of these concepts and the analytical model for understanding adaptation and change within systems.

My own interest in the application of this perspective to the study of family violence evolved from several different emphases in my work. I became attracted to the systems theory perspective early in my academic career, because it focused on the complexity and interrelatedness of whole systems. Like others, however, I was frustrated that there were few applications of this perspective within my area of specialization, the family.

My awareness of the problem of wife battering started when, in the mid-1970s, I joined one of the early task forces on family violence in my own community. I eventually became a member of a state coalition for battered women, and began to explore existing research and research opportunities as an associate of the Family Violence Research Program at the University of New Hampshire. When Mary Price, the founder of a women's shelter in a city in the northeast part of the country, contacted us at the University of New Hampshire about coordinating a research project at the shelter, I began to evaluate the advantages of this opportunity to study the processes within family systems that lead to patterns of wife battering becoming established and possibly changing over time.

This proposed sample could not fulfill the research criteria of being randomly chosen and representative of all women who had been beaten by their husbands or living partners, but this sample could help fill a void in the literature of wife beating. Population statistics and group characteristics and rates had been researched with a nationally representative sample (Straus, Gelles, & Steinmetz, 1980). The processes of interaction that surrounded the violent acts, however, had not been adequately explored. It was clear at the time that a study which focused on the processes of interaction within the family could provide insight into the dynamic aspects of wife beating. This also was an excellent opportunity to study how the man–woman relationship worked as a system. The sequence of acts and reactions surrounding each violent incident could provide qualitative data to analyze the feedback patterns that control behavior. Specifically, this could lead to an understanding of the relationship between those feedback patterns and further violence.

The way a family interacts at the time of significant events has been regarded as an indicator of the basic structure and dynamics of relationships within the family (LaRossa, 1977; Lewis, 1959; LeMasters, 1957; Caplan, 1960). It was likely that the women who would come to the shelter had been involved in a pattern of repeated violence. This offered the opportunity to focus on how that pattern became a stable part of their interaction with the men.

In addition, these women also had made an attempt to change that pattern by coming to a shelter. Thus, on the theoretical level this offered the opportunity to study how patterns do or do not change, and to discover how structural conditions and interaction processes were related to change in a family system. On the concrete level this offered the opportunity to examine many of the answers to questions asked by practitioners and policy makers. For example: Who goes to shelters? What happens to the women as a result of going to shelters? Why do women sometimes return to the men even after making a decision to come to a shelter? What happens if they do return to the men? What happens if they go out on their own? Do they again get involved in similar relationships?

Given all of these opportunities, naturally I decided to take on this research project. At the same time I accepted that this would be an intensive study of a small number of women's histories.

I quickly went about developing the outline of an exploratory intensive study. A major concern was to develop an appropriate research tool in time to include the first women who came to the shelter.

Since the women in the sample had all voluntarily sought help at a shelter for abused women, the sample is a clinical sample. Data from clinical samples cannot be generalized to larger populations. This sample does not represent either all women, or all women who have been abused. In addition, data from clinical samples are limited because what is to be explained (the dependent variable) does not vary; therefore, comparison is precluded. In this case all of the women had been beaten, and this study does not compare those who have and have not been beaten to distinguish the processes that lead to or do not lead to violence.

My task was to describe some of the processes that shape the everyday experiences of women who are beaten by their husbands or men they live with. In so doing the study may contribute to an understanding of these women's lives, to the development of new hypotheses for further research, and to the further development of a systems theoretical perspective. Despite the limitations of the study, I hope that this work will be relevant to family scholars and to other professionals and lay people interested in the problem of wife beating and in the formulation and implementation of social policy in this area.

Preparation of a monograph is a process like other social processes that is aided and frustrated by factors in the social environment. At this point I would like to forget the frustrations and acknowledge the many sources of aid, comfort, and constructive criticism.

Financial aid for this research came from the National Institute of Mental Health Grant #T32 MH 15161 to the Family Violence Research Program at the University of New Hampshire. The Texas Christian University Research Foundation provided financial support during final preparation of the manuscript.

Bert Adams, Ellen Cohn, David Finkelhor, Cathy Greenblat, Reuben Hill, Gerald Hotaling, Arnold Linsky, Donald Murray, Mary Price, Howard Shapiro, Bill Sims, Murray Straus, and Kersti Yllo all made helpful comments on the ideas presented herein. I am particularly grateful to Mary Price for making the opportunity available and to Murray Straus for identifying both fruitful areas to pursue and flawed or unclear analysis. Seymour Weingarten and Judith Grauman of The Guilford Press have provided both encouragement and constructive criticism.

Final typing fell to Janet Anthony, Phyllis Drake, Diane Brown, Marcia Caple, and Lois Cook, and I appreciate their perseverance and talent.

Last, but not least, I would like to thank the women who provided the histories presented in this volume. They generously gave their time and openly discussed their experiences. As one subject indicated, their motives were also generous: "Maybe some other women will not have to go through what I had to go through."

Contents

Introduction

Debbie's husband, Bob, had abused her. Here is how Debbie described one incident of abuse:

I was sitting over there and for no reason he came up and just knocked me over in the chair. I went down. Me and the chair went down, and he started knocking me all over the kitchen, and down the hall here, and pushed me and I scraped my arm, and he pushed me into that thing right there, and I scraped my arm real bad. I asked him if I could wash my arm off 'cause it was bleeding a little bit and he said, "No." Then I went into the bedroom, and he started knocking me around the bedroom. I was up against the door, and he slapped my face, and I hit my head on the door sill, and a big bump came up. I said, "Can I go wash my face?" and he said, "No." It scared me because a big bump just immediately arose, and that scared me. Then he knocked me down and kicked me a couple of times, and finally he just walked out. I had bruises all over me, on my face and on my arms, on my legs, and . . . I couldn't go right to work.

Elizabeth told how her man, Brad, once beat her:

He hit me, and he said, "Now you are going to hit me." I said, "No, I'm not going to hit you. I don't want to hit you." I said, "Please just leave me alone." I started crying. He did it again, and I still didn't hit back. Then he just chuckled and walked off. He never slapped me across the face, though.

I wanted to kill him, but I didn't. I just said, "Why, why is this happening to me?" It was like he wanted to punish me.

There was another time when he kicked me. He just kept kicking me. I felt angry, but I couldn't show it. I was too afraid. I don't think I felt . . . I never felt like I could strike him. I don't know if I ever could. I just didn't know how to give it back. Just couldn't do it. I'm afraid of what I would do if I did.

1

Paula described the battering relationship she had with her husband, Ed, with the following incident:

He went down in the cellar to fix the stove and I went down to try to talk to him. He wanted me to bend over so he could have sex downstairs. I said, "I don't drop my pants every time you turn around and want sex." He said, "You do what I tell you to do."

When we went back upstairs to eat, we were sitting at the table and he was saying something—"You're gonna . . ." do something. I said, "No, I don't want to," and he kicked me under the table. I said, "Don't kick me." He said, "I'll kick you if I want to. I'll do anything I want to you." Then he hit me with a stick and said I'd do anything he wanted me to because I was his property.

These are just three incidents involving three women who came to a shelter for battered women. Many other incidents are more serious. Some involve severe injury, sexual assault, and threats or attempts on women's lives. What happened to Debbie, Elizabeth, and Paula is happening to at least 1.8 million American women, by most conservative estimates (Straus, 1977a, p. 446). A large percentage of American women are physically attacked by the men with whom they live.

This work approaches the problem of battered women from their perspective. Thirty-one women who came to a shelter for battered women were interviewed in depth about their entire relationships with their men. Three of these women's histories—those of Debbie, Elizabeth, and Paula—are presented in this work to illustrate the complexity of the individual histories of battered women, and to illustrate also the similarities that may exist in the processes of battering relationships.

The abuse described by three different women personally demeaned them and often was extreme enough to cause serious injuries. One of the three still lives with her husband. He continues to beat her. Another of the three lives alone in an apartment with her children, struggles to pay the bills, and struggles to meet the emotional needs of her youngsters. The third divorced one abusing man and remarried yet another who abused her.

Two basic assumptions guide this work. The first is that *the women themselves are the only ones who can convey the complexity of their relationships.* This study presents the battered woman's perspective about the relationship. We want to understand both the individual cases and the more general processes that lead to battering behavior. Thus, the second assumption guiding this work is that if *we study the*

behavior in the context in which it takes place, we can discover general
processes which relate context and behavior in battering relationships.

Let me explain each assumption more fully.

Battered women know what it is like to live with a batterer, and
they know what it is like to try to leave a battering relationship. To
understand their histories, we must listen to the women tell their own
stories. The women's stories present their perspectives on their relationships with battering males and their perceptions of those men. The
stories are not unbiased, but the perceptions of the women are important. Those perceptions are the basis for the women's behaviors in their
relationships with men who batter them. To understand why battered
women respond as they do, and make decisions when they do, requires
knowledge of their perceptions of their own situations.

On the basis of this assumption, three of the women interviewed
present their own stories in their own words, with only minor editing
changes in those narratives. Such a method of presenting material does
have a drawback. The women may tell their stories to favor their side of
the conflict. One sees only the woman's perspective, not the man's.
Letting the women tell their own stories in as much detail as possible
seems defensible on two grounds, however. First, it would not be
ethical or practical to witness the interactions taking place over a
period of time in battering relationships; thus the recorded histories as
narrated by the women involved are a special source of data. Second, a
methodology based on preselection of variables can exclude factors that
were important to the women who actually were battered. Preselection
of variables is also guided by theoretical paradigms, and some of the
dominant theoretical paradigms have been prejudicial to women. For
example, women's problems have been analyzed as the result of an
inability to adjust to the female role, rather than the female role being
the problem (Chesler, 1971). This study thus presents the histories of
battered women in their own words and in as much detail as possible.

The second assumption is that by studying the behaviors and
contexts of battering relationships, we can discover general systems
processes related to battering behaviors. There are at least two possible
ways to approach the study of the context(s) of battering behavior. First
is a social structural viewpoint which emphasizes the discovery of
statistical associations between social structural factors and battering
behaviors of groups of subjects. The second is to look at the immediate
context in which battering behavior takes place to see how the social
structural conditions are related to an individual's behavior, and also

to see how the interaction within that immediate context regulates behavior. This study examines context from the second point of view.

As one aspect of the larger problem of family violence, wife beating is related to structural conditions such as the patriarchal nature of society, to the class structure, and to the level of violence in the society as a whole (Straus *et al.*, 1980). We know that wife beating is more likely to occur given some or all of these structural conditions, but not all men who share such structural characteristics beat their wives or living partners. To try and explain the variation, when large groups with different structural characteristics are compared, we need to refine our knowledge by looking at the immediate context of the battering behavior.

There is also a need to find out how the pattern of battering behavior evolved between specific men and women. If we take a cross-sectional slice of the population at one point in time, we find there are associations between social phenomena and battering. The process of development that has led to the behavioral correlation of specific groups of people has not been explained, however. To analyze the process requires a framework that focuses on the dynamics of behaviors in particular contexts.

When a man and woman create a relationship, that relationship consists of a relatively stable set of interacting patterns. We call that stable set a system. Looking at the patterns of interaction within the system shifts the focus from consideration of the isolated behaviors of individuals to a consideration of interaction, and to the effects of the individual's behavior on others, the reactions of others to the behavior, and the context in which behaviors take place.

Structural characteristics that may be related to battering behavior are part of the context in which the behavior takes place. Looking at the actions, the effects on others of those actions, and reactions to the behavior, however, adds a dynamic perspective to the study of that context.

The example of Paula and Ed can be analyzed briefly to see how certain structural characteristics affect the ongoing behaviors which characterize that relationship. Ed assumed he had property rights over Paula. That is a structural condition of many marriages in American society. Questions about the dynamics of this relationship include: How did the concept of property rights become an acceptable part of, or a guiding rule for, Paula and Ed's relationship? How did the rule affect Paula? How did Paula respond when Ed exercised that right by demanding sex? How might the rule have been changed? By looking closely at the sequence of events between Paula and Ed, the context in which the events took place, and the responses to key behaviors, we can begin to answer some of those questions.

Events between Elizabeth and Brad provide another example. She noted the effects of Brad's behavior on her. She indicated what her responses were. Brad's hitting and kicking made her feel angry and afraid, and she wanted to kill him, but she did not show how angry she was, how afraid she was, and she did not strike back. Brad responded by chuckling and walking away. This sequence of events raises such questions as these: What effect did Elizabeth's responses (or lack of them) have on Brad's subsequent behavior? Did this pattern of interaction lead to stabilizing violence as an ongoing pattern in the relationship? For example, we know that Elizabeth was angry and afraid. Elizabeth hypothetically could express her anger or she could suppress it. Possibly Brad's responses would be different if Elizabeth expressed her anger. Perhaps this would reduce his violence. That is an empirical question that can be answered by looking at the dynamic sequence of events that take place between Brad and Elizabeth.

Analyzing the dynamic interaction between the people in a battering relationship can help answer many important questions that have been raised. There are several conceptual tools that make this kind of analysis easier. The conceptual tools that will be used in this study to analyze histories of battered women who came to a shelter are based on Buckley's (1967) application of modern systems theory to sociology. In Chapter 1, I will look at Buckley's description of a system and the systems concepts of boundaries, positive and negative feedback processes, open versus closed systems, thresholds of viability within systems, smaller systems within the larger sociocultural system, and finally systems in transition. As the concepts are defined, I will suggest the relevance of such concepts to the study of wife beating.

The theoretical concepts of a systems approach have been used in the family area, particularly in the study of conflict, but there has been little systematic use of these concepts in the research specifically on family violence. Chapter 2 provides a theoretical and empirical background for the integration of literature on wife battering with work that has been done by family scholars using systems theory. Integrating these areas provides a framework for the analysis of the women's histories in later chapters.

To understand these women's lives, and the processes that led to the patterns of violence, requires a longitudinal perspective. This volume presents two types of longitudinal analyses. The first type compares retrospective data on the history of 31 violent relationships; in-depth interviews with 31 battered women, who had voluntarily sought help at a shelter, provide the histories. These include information on their early family background, that of their partners, and the history of their relationships.

The second type of longitudinal analysis compares violence patterns in the year preceding the women's stay in the shelter (time 1), with the patterns of violence in the six months after they came to the shelter (time 2). Of the original 31 women, 24 were reinterviewed six months after their stay at the shelter to provide a basis for this analysis.

Chapter 3 presents a description of the demographic and social characteristics of these women, as well as quantitative comparisons of levels of violence, and key aspects of the history of violence.

Chapter 3 also includes an analysis of circumstances surrounding three incidents of violence. Specific questions are analyzed concerning marital status at the time, the sequence of events, and responses to the incidents. To provide a measure of change over time, I asked the same questions about each of the three incidents.

This research is unique. It presents a longitudinal analysis and integrates both quantitative and qualitative data. The qualitative data are presented in the form of three life histories in Chapters 4, 5, and 6. These data are presented in the form of life histories, or what many qualitative researchers call a person's "career." These life histories focus on the sequence of changes both in the relationship(s) with their primary partners, and the changing definitions of self the women have had at various stages in those relationships.

Chapter 7 has a process model of stability and change in wife-battering relationships using general systems theory concepts. This model synthesizes both the quantitative and the qualitative data from the study into a model to describe the processes that govern the patterns of violence over time.

The first part of Chapter 7 describes a six-stage model of wife battering. The second part presents a flow chart to illustrate the cybernetic and morphogenic processes that contribute to change or stability over time.

CHAPTER 1

A Systems Theory Perspective

Family sociologists have become increasingly interested in the family as a social system (Broderick & Smith, 1979; Hill, 1971; Kantor & Lehr, 1975; Straus, 1973). This approach offers a conceptual framework that focuses on processes at several different levels.

One difficulty with understanding systems theory is the complexity of the components of the framework. The purpose of this chapter is to explore a definition of systems, the concepts that are necessary to understand that framework, and to discuss the different levels in the structure of feedback and control within systems.

The first part of this chapter focuses on Buckley's description of a system and the key systems concepts of boundaries, positive and negative feedback processes, open versus closed systems, thresholds of viability within systems, smaller systems within the larger sociocultural system, and finally systems in transition. As the concepts are defined, I will suggest the relevance of these concepts to the study of wife battering.

In addition this chapter includes a discussion of Broderick and Smith's (1979) hierarchies of feedback and control. These hierarchies theoretically describe how the system monitors and corrects its responses to meet its goals or to change those goals.

A SYSTEM

I shall not define the general concept of a "system," but rather concentrate on describing the nature of systems in terms of structural arrangements and patterns of interaction. Buckley (1967), in his argument for systems theory as a more viable and appropriate framework than outmoded models of society, describes a system as follows:

The kind of system we are interested in may be described generally as a complex of elements or components directly or indirectly related in a causal network, such that each component is related to at least some others in a more or less stable way within any particular period of time. The components may be relatively simple and stable, or complex and changing; they may vary in only one or two properties or take on many different states. The interrelations between them may be mutual or unidirectional, linear, non-linear or intermittent, and varying in degrees of causal efficacy or priority. The particular kinds of more or less stable interrelationships of components that become established at any time constitute the particular structure of the system at that time, thus achieving a kind of "whole" with some degree of continuity and boundary. (p. 41)

The components of the system are not related in a simple cause-and-effect way. The response to an act may also be a cause in the ongoing pattern of interrelationships. A simple example is the husband and wife each of whom complains about the other. He complains that she nags him, and she complains that he withdraws. If we looked at a tape of their interaction, we would see that the sequence of her nagging and his withdrawal could be divided at the point where she nags and he responds by withdrawing, or at the point where he withdraws and she nags (Watzlawick *et al.*, 1967, pp. 54–60). Deciding the cause and the effect depends on how one divides the sequence. Division may be a totally arbitrary act, and it may be more realistic to look at each of their responses as the precipitant to the next act of the other. The causal analysis in this example could then show the interrelatedness of both of their behaviors.

In addition, the patterns of interrelating within established systems tend to become somewhat stabilized. They may be highly stabilized or they may be less stabilized and thus changing. Different systems may differ in the degree of stability and change. A particular system may go through periods of stability followed by periods of change, or the reverse. The Amish culture is an example of a system that has relatively stable home and family relationships over a period of time. If group members leave the closed community, however, they are presented with many new stimuli and opportunities. When they return, the group may go through a period of change and adjustment. This is one reason why the Amish attempt to restrict outside contact.

Conceptualizing the battering relationship as a system means that we can look at the process of actions and reactions as a continuous causal chain, each reaction becoming in turn a precipitant. We can also look at a system to find the periods of stability and change, and identify the processes that took place during those different times to produce stability or change.

Systems have boundaries that define where the system begins and ends, and what information or behavior is an acceptable part of that system. Any behavior that deviates from the ongoing pattern of behavior or that challenges the boundaries of the system triggers a response. The nature of the response is governed by how the new behavior fits with the goals of the particular system, or the particular components of the system. An example of the processes working between couples is included in the excerpt of Paula and Ed's interaction which is quoted in the Introduction. Ed's demand for sex and Paula's compliance had been an established part of their relationship until this episode. Ed expected Paula to go along as she had before. This time she said no, and the response was a new behavior on her part. Ed could have said, "Okay, you have a right to say no if you don't want sex," or he could do as he did and tell her she had no right to say no because she was his property. Because Ed's apparent goal was to maintain his property rights, he responded by reasserting his authority instead of accepting Paula's refusal. Even though Paula did not go along with having sex at that point, Ed reasserted his dominance both verbally and later up in the kitchen with physical violence. This sequence of events tended to reestablish the pattern of his dominance. If he had said "Okay," this would have been new behavior to which Paula could have responded according to her own goals. If Paula's response had been accepted by Ed, the stable pattern of his asserting dominance and Paula's compliance would have changed. The new behavior would theoretically have set off a chain of reactions and adjustments because the components of the system are related in a mutually causal way.

POSITIVE AND NEGATIVE FEEDBACK

Responses to new behavior are called feedback because the response conveys information to the first member of the system about how the preceding acts, bits of information, gestures, or other communications are received. New input into a system represents deviation from the stabilized, ongoing pattern. Because the new input is different, it triggers a response that may discourage or encourage new behavior.

Negative Feedback Tends to Reduce the Likelihood
New Behavior Will Occur Again

In the case of Paula and Ed, Ed's actual response represented negative feedback to Paula's new behavior of saying no. His response made it less likely Paula would try to say no again than if he had said "Okay."

Positive Feedback Tends to Support New Behavior

The information conveyed (whether intentionally or not) is that the new behavior is acceptable or effective within the system. If Ed had said "Okay," Paula would have been more likely to say no again when the demand for sex did not coincide with her own desire for sex. Positive feedback to new behavior allows new behavior into the system and thus sets in motion change in other parts of the system. Maybe Paula's saying no would precipitate change in Ed to be more considerate or kind in his approaches to sex.

OPEN VERSUS CLOSED SYSTEMS

Systems that have the same characteristics and the same boundaries over a long period of time remain in static equilibrium. These systems can be called closed because they do not adapt to changes in the outside environment. Boundaries exist between the system and the outside social environment. Sometimes these boundaries are natural phenomena such as the thick jungle that remained for many generations as the boundary between the isolated Tasaday tribe of the Philippines and the rest of civilization. At other times the boundaries may be created by system rules. An example is the deliberate attempt of the Amish to keep destructive influences from their young—they have no televisions and Amish children do not attend public schools.

No social systems are completely closed. All systems exist on a continuum from open to closed. At the extreme of openness, the system is entirely open to input from the outside. Most social systems are adaptive; there is gradual change and development over a period of time.

The degree of openness and closedness is related to the amount of change in a social system. In general, the more open the system, the more change, and the more closed the system, the more stable the patterns of behavior—the less the system changes. This concept may help us understand change in patterns of wife beating in a man–woman system or systems of couples. In a relatively closed system we would expect to find highly repetitive patterns of behavior and a high degree of negative feedback to new behavior. If the system is relatively open to input from the outside social system, then the impact of social norms that discourage severe abuse may be felt sooner, and change may occur in that pattern. An important question is whether different types of systems created by couples in battering relationships produced patterns of violence of different duration or frequency. This is a question I will try to answer by studying histories of battered women and the context in which a battering took place.

THE THRESHOLD OF VIABILITY

Systems are interrelated networks which tend to maintain themselves by regulating the amount of stability and change. This regulation takes place through the process of positive and negative feedback. Generally individual systems maintain consistent levels of stability and change over long periods of time. When crises occur, or when there is change in the environment in which the system exists, the internal regulation of the system may be disrupted.

To remain viable, systems require some stability and some adaptive change. Individual systems may have patterns of behavior that have become stabilized, and even though patterns of behavior may be destructive to individual members—patterns of violence, for example— the system has adapted to those behaviors and is still a viable system.

To change behavior patterns that have become stabilized within the system requires some new input. For example, let us suppose that beatings have been happening over time on a routine basis and the woman has adapted to the beatings by withdrawal, suppression of feelings, or possibly displacement of the anger onto children or others. In that case, the system that includes this stable pattern of interaction is unlikely to change without input from some other source that presents some new information. This new information could be some social program intervention, some new opportunity, some supportive new alliance of one of the members of the system, or the openness of one member to some new perspective.

All of the women in the present study left their abusive husbands or partners at least temporarily. Did the event of leaving reflect the reaching of a threshold of viability in a battering relationship system? At what point did the system no longer seem viable for the women? What made the women leave when they did? How were they able to do that? What social circumstances might have made it possible for them to leave at that time? These questions may be answered by looking at the detailed events surrounding the women's moves. From this kind of study, we may be able to discover ways to help other women make moves to change patterns of abuse in their relationships. Perhaps it will also add to our knowledge of how the family operates as a social system.

SYSTEMS IN A SOCIAL ENVIRONMENT

Families exist as systems within the large sociocultural system. The family is both influenced by larger social conditions and influences that larger social system. Impact from the larger social system can involve immediate changes (e.g., loss of a job), or it can involve more constant and pervasive elements—for example, socially established sex roles, racial relations, economic, or power relations within the sociocultural system, and others. Family behavior also can influence the larger social system. For example, if families keep behavior such as violent behavior strictly private and do not reveal its existence to police, doctors, friends, neighbors, or others, then the larger social system will be largely ignorant of the problem and unequipped to deal with it satisfactorily when it is revealed. If the behavior is not revealed, the tendency of the larger social system will be to regard it as idiosyncratic, and probably as evidence of personal disturbance. This may help explain why so many professionals have used a personal disturbance model as the basis for dealing with such cases. If violence is not revealed as a common occurrence in families, neither professionals nor others will regard it as a societal problem and look for solutions within the social structure.

Macrolevel social conditions are related to patterns of wife beating. An example is the high incidence of violence among the unemployed (Straus et al., 1980). The question left unanswered is, how does unemployment impact on families? We presume that unemployment occurs as a result of social conditions and that unemployment affects the families. There is another possibility—that family or individual problems can lead to unemployment. Both of these possibilities can be studied by looking at histories of couples involved in a violent relationship.

The social environment can produce stress on the family, but that environment also can provide supports. Extended kin networks are associated with lower rates of violence in at least one study, and the possibility exists that other social supports can effectively reduce violence rates or keep them low or nonexistent. The impact of the larger social system on the family and the family on the social system may both be important to the understanding of wife beating.

SYSTEMS IN TRANSITION

All of the women interviewed for this study have come to a shelter for battered women. Many have returned to their husbands or living partners after their stay at the shelter, but all of them can be considered in the process of transition or change. The only difference among the women is the amount of change or how much of a transition they are going through.

Because systems are relatively stable over a period of time, transitions require adaptation to many changes. Other transitions that have been studied are the transition to becoming married, to having a first child, to a divorce, to the empty-nest stage of life, to aging, and to death. These other studies of critical periods of transition or adjustments indicate that when people are going through transitions they are particularly vulnerable to physical and emotional problems. Studies also indicate that factors such as social support and prior histories of coping with problems affect how people deal with major life transitions.

Loss of a relationship often is experienced as loss of part of oneself, and the greater the interdependence of the two people in the relationship, the greater the feelings of loss. The transition from a relationship with an abusive man may result in the woman facing many new problems. For example, it may be that leaving an abusive husband may raise issues a woman hasn't faced before—being a single parent, getting financial support for herself and her children, or dealing with such stigmatizing labels as "divorcee," and seeking to establish a new male-female relationship. It is important to understand what the transition is like for the woman trying to leave a battering relationship.

Since many women who come to shelters do not permanently leave their husbands, it also is important to know what the transition back into a relationship is like for those who do return. This may involve returning to the same interrelated patterns of behavior that occurred before. Change in those patterns of interaction also may occur. Studying these cases may lead to insights about ways to change those patterns.

HIERARCHIES OF FEEDBACK AND CONTROL

Having discussed the various components of a systems theory perspective, attention will now be directed to the levels at which feedback operates and the effect of four different levels of feedback on the system. This discussion stems from Broderick and Smith's (1979) explication of this theoretical perspective.

Broderick and Smith (1979) have isolated three different hierarchies that describe rules of system transformation. These are "strata" hierarchies, "temporal/logical" hierarchies, and hierarchies of feedback and control. Strata hierarchies refer to the level of system analysis. For example, within a family, each member has his/her own intrapsychic system which may include patterns of response learned earlier in the primary family backgrond. In addition, there is an interpersonal system including all members of that system. Of course the number of members may change over time producing changes in that system. The most classic examples of such changes are when a child is born, a family member dies, or a couple is divorced. Finally, the family system is affected by each member as part of perhaps multiple other systems such as extended family systems or work systems.

Temporal/logical hierarchies refer to the sequence of steps that occur to produce output. If members of the system go through steps that are provided in the system of rules, they can be relatively certain of the output and the response of other members of the system.

Hierarchies of feedback and control refer to the levels at which the feedback operates to monitor the system's progress toward a goal. Level I is simple feedback, a circular process by which output is subsequently processed as an input. The second level is the level that is often compared with the thermostat that controls the heating unit. This is "Level II: Cybernetic Control." There is a monitoring unit at this level which processes all input to discern if the input is consistent with the goals of the system. In family systems, the goals of the system include rules for appropriate behaviors, established boundaries of interaction, and patterns that have been dominant over time. If new input challenges the goals of the system, corrective action usually occurs. Different systems have different degrees of openness or closedness to new input, but even if the system appears to be very open, corrective action would take place if a member of that system acted in a way that was inconsistent with the family rules.

The rules of the system are not always set by consensus within the system. If one member of the system is more powerful, his/her own personal goals prevail over goals of the total system. In the case of Ed and Paula, his rules about ownership dominated the system. The fact that Ed's rules dominated the system for several years, maybe even for the entire length of their relationship, gives those rules the added force of being the established pattern.

This raises the question of how rules could be changed over time. The first step in that process is the realization that occurs when corrective action at the second level does not work. In the case of Ed and Paula, his attempt to correct her when she refused to comply with his wishes may have worked or not worked to reassert his property rights. If it worked, no change in the system would occur. If it did not work, however, there is theoretically a possibility for change.

This third level of feedback control is "Level III: Morphogenesis" (Broderick & Smith, 1979). At this level the corrective action has not succeeded at reestablishing equilibrium, and each member of the system may try alternative responses.

In the case of a violent couple, this is an important part of establishing a violent pattern. For example, either partner may get more violent to establish or maintain his/her power position, and in turn a higher level of violence becomes a part of the family system.

This process is also important when one member of the system wants to change that pattern by escaping the violence. For example, if the woman has been able to control the amount of violence in the past by pacifying the man, but at some point this no longer works or her definition of what is acceptable behavior changes, she is likely to try to seek help from others. This commonly occurs when women try to get out of battering relationships. They talk to family, friends, clergy, physicians, counselors, and police. This initially represents a new effort to correct the stability in the system. Most women in this study initially sought help from others outside the home in order to control the man, not to leave the system.

Failure of these efforts to reestablish control in the home may lead to changes in the structure of the system as a whole. This level of feedback control is labeled "Level IV: Reorientation or Conversion" by Broderick and Smith (1979).

At lower levels, the structure and basic goals of the system have not been challenged. At this level, however, there is the potential for a different kind of morphogenesis. This level is extremely important in the histories of battered women.

Once patterns have been established and operating for long periods of time, they are extremely resistant to change. The type of change that is possible in more flexible systems that are open to small changes in input, is not usually possible after wife battering has occurred for long periods of time.

There are several implications here for a theoretical understanding of wife battering. The first is that different processes may govern change after one incident, than after several incidents. Second, minor corrective mechanisms may not be adequate to stop violence after it has been established. Minor corrective mechanisms on the part of the man may not be enough to reestablish the family system once a woman has sought outside help. For the family system to continue at all may require more fundamental restructuring. This is a difficult task in any established system of behavior.

As Broderick and Smith (1979) indicate, the investigation of change at this level requires longitudinal analysis. This is often difficult, particularly in the family violence area. However, retrospective accounting of change that has taken place can provide some insight into the nature of processes in family systems, and the conditions that are necessary for change to occur.

In the present study, women have reconstructed the history of their relationship with the man. These data will be used to analyze the conditions under which violence became an established pattern, and under what conditions the women in this study who had all attempted to change the system by leaving were able to do this.

In addition, the women were interviewed on two different occasions to determine if change had taken place. These two types of longitudinal data provide a unique basis for understanding wife battering from a systems theory approach.

CHAPTER 2

Theoretical and Empirical Background to a Systems Theory Approach to Wife Battering

Previous research on the general area of conflict, and the more specific area of wife battering, provides both theoretical and empirical background for the analysis of stability and change in battering relationships. Previous research has approached the area of wife battering from two basically different perspectives. One approach focuses on finding linear–causal explanations for the question of *why* wife battering occurs. The other uses a systems theory approach, focusing on the process of conflict and *how* wife battering occurs.

Using a linear–causal approach, researchers have noted the occurrence of wife battering and searched for a preceding cause. Possible causes investigated have been intrapsychic phenomena such as instincts, inborn biological drives, psychological frustration, and observable conditions of the social structure, that is, legal institutions, sex-role stereotyping, socialization patterns, and power relations between members of a couple.

Looking for the causes of wife battering within persons reflects the view that social patterns and institutionalized behaviors are the result of personal traits held by many people at the same time. Looking for the causes of wife battering in the social structure reflects the view that the social structural conditions determine behavior in a cause–effect relationship.

Both of these attempts to find linear–causal relationships have recently been challenged by general systems theory.

> It has become apparent that we must question both the view that institutional structure is "only" personal association writ large, and on the other hand, that institutional structure "molds" the situation of action as well as personality to the extent of determining behavior beyond a minimal residue of choice and decision-making that is unique and innovative. (Buckley, 1967, p. 127)

A general systems theory approach, assumes that discrete cause–effect analyses cannot capture the complexity of social behavior. Instead of linear cause–effect explanation, general systems theory focuses on the complexity of mutually causal events.

Systems theory focuses on the processes that occur, and the interrelationships between events, people, or other elements of the system. The presence and level of a pattern of behavior such as wife battering results from ongoing patterns of interaction within the system.

Instead of searching for a linear–causal explanation of wife battering, general systems theory focuses on the question of *how* violence develops over time to the level of wife battering, and *how* the wife battering becomes an ongoing pattern resistant to change.

We think on the basis of "how" questions a lot of the time. For example, we ask "How does digestion occur?" rather than "What causes digestion?" (Scherer, Abeles, & Fischer, 1975, p. 259). As this example illustrates, we ask "how" questions when we are studying complex interrelated systems—in this case, the human body. A question such as "How does digestion occur?" focuses attention on the ongoing processes, as opposed to some prior causal condition. The distinction between "how" and "why" questions is an oversimplification, in that systems analysis also is concerned with causes.

Social systems are complex interrelated networks of mutually causal elements with relatively stable patterns of relationships. Systems theory interprets cause–effect links as elements in a cycle of behavior, which includes continuing feedback responses, and behavioral reactions. The addition to the traditional cause–effect model is the area of responses, conceptualized as feedback. The study of feedback can potentially explain some behavior that cause–effect models cannot. For example, we know that those people who were abused as children have higher rates of abusing their own children or their spouses than those people who were not abused as children (Straus *et al.*, 1980). A cause–

effect interpretation suggests that being abused as a child causes one to abuse one's own child or one's spouse. However, not all people who were abused as children abuse their children or beat their spouses. Some that were not abused as children do abuse their children and/or their spouses. Abuse or nonabuse, therefore, is not completely determined by the earlier behavior. A theoretical gap exists to explain these cases.

To solve this theoretical gap, it is important to understand the processes leading to the earlier pattern which is repeated in later generations (or is not repeated). The questions "How does violence occur in all relationships?" and "How does violence occur in relationships where the parent was abused as a child?" shift the focus to processes over time within complex sets of relationships. This level of analysis opens up the opportunity for a more subtle and complex understanding.

The general systems theory approach suggests new areas of explanation to develop a more complete theory of how wife battering arises and how it becomes stabilized or changes over time. The theoretical background for a systems theory approach lies in theories of process, social change, and symbolic interactionism. The interactionism school of sociology has been important to the development of the concept of process. Early interactionism models first challenged the static models of society (Buckley, 1967). Within this theoretical perspective, there have been a number of classical studies of social change and social control. This school of sociology views social change as the product of the system, not of individual member's characteristics. For example, deviance is seen as the product of structuring processes within the sociocultural system which define some behavior as deviant even within highly conforming societies (Becker, 1963; Erikson, 1966; Goffman, 1961; Scheff, 1966). These studies of deviance focus on labeling and role fulfillment according to the rules of the social system.

Labeling theories of deviance can be adapted to the study of violent behavior (Straus, 1973). A general systems theory of family violence assumes that violence is the outcome of the complex social interaction within the family system which exists as part of a larger social system.

The study of family communication patterns reveals how the processes of rule formation and structuring patterns control family members' behavior (Bateson, 1972; Haley, 1963; Jackson, 1957; Watzlawick et al., 1967). Clinical experiences with schizophrenic patients led to observations of how members of the patient's family encouraged and even seemed to demand that the patient remain ill. These observations led to a focus on the family's systematic patterns of interaction.

Theories that focus on how the system contributes to ill-behavior assume that the initial "deviant behavior" results from a combination of learning and response patterns to slightly unusual behavior that may have occurred by random chance. They also focus on how the family acted as a governor to control behavior that deviated from the established ongoing behavior, encouraged the behavior, and led to the behavior-problem member of the family maintaining that particular pattern of response.

Because mentally ill patients have established patterns of deviant behavior, most observations of their family systems focused on homeostatic processes (Watzlawick et al., 1967). The aim of therapy, however, is to change the behavior. Family therapy developed as a form of therapy for treating these cases, because it is difficult to change an individual family member's behavior without changing ongoing processes in the whole family.

The early work on family systems was marked by the limitation of clinical samples. The stimulating ideas of this early work, however, led to the study of "normal" families. For example, families were studied in a laboratory to see how they interacted as a system when presented with different tasks (Reiss, 1971). From this research we learned how families differ in the way members react to each other and in relation to information from the environment outside the family. Families differ based on the nature of family interaction. Some families are relatively "open" and sensitive to input from each other and from the environment outside the family. Others are more closed to input from each other or "constrained" and reluctant to acknowledge input that may produce change (Reiss, 1971). Families have somewhat unique structuring processes of communication which control what happens within that family and also control the relationship of the family to the larger social system.

In naturalistic settings—individual family homes—families also exhibit differences in how they structure interaction within the family and with outsiders. On the basis of research in individual family homes, Kantor and Lehr (1975) typed families as closed, open, or random, based on the boundaries of the family system. Boundaries circumscribe the areas where relationships and information are sought, accepted, and processed. Boundaries are narrow and rigidly maintained in the closed family. Most of the communication is regulated by constancy or negative feedback loops which leads to stabile patterns of interaction over time. Open families choose a mixture of equilibrium and disequilibrium, and have periods of both constancy and change. Random families have fluctuating patterns of interrelationships as well as boundaries.

Each of these types is viable and results from the self-direction of the family system according to the goals of that system. This approach implies that there is no one ideal family pattern. Each pattern has its potential problem areas. This approach emphasizes how specific patterns of behavior become stabilized and how feedback processes affect specific behavioral responses. This focus on how system processes affect behavior has implications for the study of conflict.

A SYSTEMS THEORY APPROACH TO CONFLICT

A systems theory approach to conflict raises two questions: (1) What is the process of conflict within a family system, and (2) What are the effects of different system characteristics on the process of conflict?

Conflict may be inevitable in couple or family relationships (Sprey, 1969). According to this view, harmony is both the exception and may, in fact, be more problematic than normal. When two or more people are in close proximity and share common goals and resources, as people do in families, conflict results from the discrepancy between idealized expectations and the reality of scarce resources and different personal goals. If conflict is inevitable, what must be studied is how conflict is managed by couples or families (Sprey, 1969). This study must include the context of the family conflict—the larger social system.

In an empirical study of how couples handled and resolved marital conflicts, Raush, Berry, Hertel, and Swain (1974) found that conflict behavior tended to be reciprocated, and that rejection tended to elicit either emotional appeals or coercive tactics. The first of these findings suggests that conflict escalates because of the behavioral reciprocity couples exhibit. The second part of these findings suggests that when one person is rejecting, the other person within the system acts in a way to constrain the partner from leaving in order to perpetuate the system despite conflict. Couples that have more conflict tend to let conflict accumulate over time and to use tactics that are person rather than issue oriented. Couples with less conflict have shorter conflicts and tend to be more issue oriented. The couples with more conflict tended to fight about their relationship more, which indicates how strong the tendency is to try to maintain an on going family system. Over time, couples in the Raush *et al.* study used less "brinksmanship" or rejection, but the intensity of coercive tactics did not decrease. From a systems theory perspective, the maintenance of the system becomes more important over time than specific conflicts.

Males and females may differ in the way they handle conflict, but the instrumental–expressive dichotomy appears to be an overly simplistic way to describe those differences. In Raush *et al.*'s study, the authors found that early in the marriage relationship, the husband reciprocated resolution efforts of the wife, and the wife reciprocated coercive acts in the face of the husband's coercion. However, couples using different types of conflict management—for example, avoidance versus engagement—did not differ in the level of marital stability. A style of conflict management had evolved early in the family system, and once established did not contribute to differences in changes of system stability. Marriages that have stable long-enduring patterns of conflict can also be stable marriages (Cuber & Harroff, 1965).

Specific patterns of communication become part of the system of interaction and relatively resistant to change. The interaction between George and Martha in the Edward Albee play *Who's Afraid of Virginia Woolf?* illustrates this point (Watzlawick *et al.*, 1967). What goes on between them, Martha as she reacts to George and he to her, illustrates processes of feedback, in particular how positive feedback processes encourage escalation of conflict, and how negative feedback processes counteract the movement toward change (Watzlawick *et al.*, 1967, p. 153).

George and Martha arrive at a point of symmetrical escalation through positive feedback cycles which become larger and larger. Neither side in the conflict achieves a victory, however, and there is no resolution. The patterns of interaction George and Martha have evolved operate under definite rules. For example, one of their rules is the use of the mythical son to maintain some stability in their relationship.

> The primary requirement of interaction about the son is a coalition between George and Martha; they must be together on this fiction in order to maintain it for, unlike a real child who, once procreated, exists, here they must constantly unite to create their child. And, changing the focus slightly, in this one area they can get together, collaborating without competition. . . . There is a built-in limit to their game of symmetrical escalation in the necessity to share this fiction. Their child-myth is a homeostatic mechanism. (Watzlawick *et al.*, 1967, p. 174)

By maintaining one important area of mutual concern in which they cooperate, George and Martha reestablish equilibrium for their marital system. In their case the area is a myth-child. We might ask "What other types of behavior serve a similar or equivalent function?"

George and Martha face a problem when the myth threatens to explode before their guests. At that point Martha takes a one-down conciliatory position; George slaps her hand, grabs her hair, and pulls her head back. Mutual escalation stops, although the battle is not over. The two then become close to breaking their own patterns, but in the end a conciliatory move is made and the system maintains itself.

The Albee play is fiction, but it provides an exciting vehicle for the sequential analysis of systems processes. Analyses may not be so neat when we deal with real systems, but they may be more particularly informing. LaRossa (1977) provides an example of an analysis that is both theoretically based and also focused on a particular problem.

In a study of how the husband–wife system worked during the first pregnancy stage, LaRossa found that conflict became a prominent factor. On the basis of this study LaRossa claims that contemporary marriage is a system that can be analyzed according to a conflict paradigm with the power structure as the control center of the system. There are essentially two aspects of this power structure: the environmental power and exchange structure, and the marital power and exchange structure. As in Scanzoni's work (1970), LaRossa discusses how these two aspects of the power structure are intimately related. The marital symbol structure, which is the set of privately and mutually understood, agreed-upon and not agreed-upon symbols, is related to the marital exchange structure which includes the rewards and costs bestowed by the couple on each other in a mutually causal way.

LaRossa's model does not extend to the analysis of systems processes of feedback or to the patterns of homeostasis versus morphogenesis that characterize systems processes, but it does draw attention to the question of "how" conflict occurs in family systems.

To study the process of conflict from a systems theory perspective suggests looking at conflict as the ongoing interaction between members of a system. Viewing conflict in this way, it is important to either observe the ongoing process or to recreate the events from natural histories. As discussed earlier, it is not ethically or practically possible to observe ongoing patterns of conflict. Natural histories, however, do provide a unique opportunity to study processes over time. To facilitate understanding the regularities of conflict processes, several questions can be used as a basis of analysis of natural histories. These include: (1) Do conflicts tend to follow the same course most times they occur? (2) Is the course of the conflict predictable based on patterns of feedback control? (3) Can the patterns of feedback control be identified and isolated as regular system processes?

In a study of natural histories of revolutions, Scherer *et al.* (1975) found that the conflict process typically proceeded through several definable stages. They also found that system processes of feedback controlled the nature of the conflict process itself. This analysis led to the description of the following stages:

> Stage 1. Precompetition. At this point, the parties have a cooperative relationship or are relatively independent.
>
> Stage 2. Competition. The system changes (due to internal historical dynamics or to events in its environment) so that the parties are in a competitive relationship.
>
> Stage 3. Conflict. The parties attack each other. What has occurred as competition and conflict has intensified as escalation. Escalation involves not only an increase in mutual punishment but also, in most systems, polarization.
>
> Escalation is a "positive feedback" process in which each event inten-sifies its own precursors. Besides these reactions, there are other changes in the system brought about by the conflict which intensify that very con-flict. Positive relationships between the sides are destroyed, the damage of battle becomes grounds for further battle, the most conflict-oriented sub-elements become dominant in each party, and polarization occurs.
>
> Stage 4. "Crisis." This is an ambiguous term and we cannot do much to clarify it, but there appears to be in many conflicts a special period when a turn is reached. It is distinguished by a new, intense, and different level of interaction, and it is when violence is most likely to occur.
>
> Stage 5. Resolution—or Revolution. The turning point or period usually means a resolution or a "revolution." The resolution can be immediate, or it can be a gradual de-escalation, but in either case, it involves a return to cooperation, or, at least competition. Another possibility is revolution in the sense that the system is drastically restructured. (Scherer *et al.*, 1975, pp. 270–274)

This model focuses on the processes that shape the natural histories of revolutions, but a similar analysis could be made of the natural histories of conflict between members of a family system. Conflict within a family is a system process that is controlled by the negative and positive feedback mechanisms. Over time, the natural history of that system can be analyzed using the same principles of systems theory as were used in the above example.

SYSTEMS THEORY AND WIFE-BATTERING RESEARCH

A systems theory of wife battering raises several questions:

1. Why does wife battering occur?
2. How does wife battering occur in relationships?
3. What forces in society or within families lead to stability in patterns of wife battering?
4. What forces in society or within families lead to change in patterns of wife battering?

Each of these questions needs to be addressed.

Why Does Wife Battering Occur?

The application of linear–causal models to the study of wife battering involves noting the occurrence of wife battering and searching for the causes. Some researchers have looked for the causes of wife beating within the individual participants, others in psychological states such as frustration, and the more sociological researchers have looked for the causes in observable conditions in the social structure.

The view that the cause of the violence is within the individual is consistent with the lay view. Committing an act of violence is seen by many as evidence that one is "crazy." The widespread acceptance of this view is related to the value placed on theories of personality as explanations for social behavior. People have a tendency to want simple answers to questions that cannot be explained easily.

Clinical studies of wife battering have contributed to another common view, the view that women who are battered have psychological problems that explain the battering. Snell, Rosenwald, and Robey (1964) studied 12 husbands and wives who had long histories of violent interaction. The wives in these cases were middle-class women who had filed charges of assault and battery, and the court had referred these couples to a psychiatrist for help. Snell and his associates interviewed both the husband and the wife, but the research report published from this study focuses primarily on the wife and her role in perpetuating or, essentially, causing the abuse. Snell and his associates concluded that the women were aggressive, masculine, had a need to dominate, were sexually frigid, and/or masochistic. This report asserts, at least by implication, that these characteristics were reason enough for any man to assert himself through violence.

The Snell *et al.* (1964) study illustrates the clinical fallacy; that is, since some women seeing a psychiatrist could be characterized as having psychiatric problems that caused the men to be violent, then by implication all women somehow bring on their own abuse. Shainess (1977) also indicates that wives almost inevitably play a part in their own assault. Shainess, however, goes on to say that the women are not to blame for it. Shainess (1977) looks at both the personality traits of battered wives and wife batterers. Wife batterers are considered to be (1) passive–aggressive, (2) obsessive–compulsive, (3) paranoid, and/or (4) sadistic. These typologies of male or female behavior are descriptions of clinical cases. They are not necessarily meant to be assertions of the causes of wife battering, but it is easy to make the leap to saying that men beat their wives *because* they are passive–aggressive, paranoid, or have some other quality or trait. This kind of descriptive explanation does not explain violence, however. The behavior of wife batterers may be described, but men who do not beat their wives may have the same characteristics. Without a comparison group, this question cannot be answered.

Psychologists assert that a variety of psychological conditions underlie the battering problem: immature personalities, personality disorders, in particular dependency and aggressiveness, jealousy reactions, addictions, and other psychiatric illnesses (Scott, 1974).

These researchers maintain that the cause of the abuse lies in the individual personalities of either the batterer or the battered wife. This type of theoretical explanation focuses on a single intrapsychic phenomenon disregarding processes of interaction and ways the social structure shapes behavior.

Experimental psychologists and the pragmatic school of psychiatry have attempted to shift focus away from intrapsychic processes and to focus on observable input–output or stimulus–response relations. They employ the "black box" concept which disregards the internal structure and concentrates on the study of specific input–output relations.

> This concept, if applied to psychological and psychiatric problems, has the heuristic advantage that no ultimately unverifiable intrapsychic hypotheses need to be invoked, and that one can limit oneself to observable

input–output relations, that is, to communication. Such an approach, we believe, characterizes an important recent trend in psychiatry toward viewing symptoms as one kind of input into the family system rather than as an expression of intrapsychic conflict. (Watzlawick *et al.*, 1967, p. 43–44)

Grounded in behaviorism and deterministic models, Dollard, Doob, Miller, Mowrer, and Sears (1939) began the search for laws of relationships between cause and effect to explain violent behavior. Their famous frustration–aggression hypothesis has stimulated many other experimental research projects (e.g., Miller, 1941; Berkowitz, 1962). The format of those experiments was to induce frustration by the manipulation of the access to goals. Aggressive behavior was observed as the dependent variable. Those studies documented the strength of the relationship between frustration and aggression, but the problem of what led to aggression as the response rather than other possible responses was never answered. Several important questions have been raised about this approach by Gelles and Straus (1979, p. 562):

Although the frustration–aggression theory is credible and seems intuitively valid, there are some major problems with the theory as currently stated. First, it does not explain under what conditions frustration leads to aggression [Etzioni, 1971, p. 717]. Second, in some societies frustration is followed by passive withdrawal [Mead & MacGregor, 1951, p. 176]. Lastly, the theory does not differentiate physical aggression from verbal abuse and aggression [Etzioni, 1971, p. 717].

For a refined explanation of a man hitting his wife or living partner, more is necessary than the explanation of frustration. This is best illustrated by thinking of the frustrations inherent in enduring man–woman relationships. Although frustration may precede most hitting, all frustrating circumstances do not lead to hitting. The frustration-aggression hypothesis, and the instinct theory of aggressive behavior are both based on the Freudian assumption that aggression is an instinctual inclination and not amenable to elimination (Bandura, 1973). This assumption is rejected by social learning theorists. "Human aggression is a learned conduct that like other forms of social behavior is under stimulus, reinforcement, and cognitive control" (Bandura, 1973, p. 44). Determinants of aggression can be found in social practices. A social learning model of aggression focuses on (1) conditions under which frustrations may lead to aggression, (2) the processes that encourage the learning of aggression, and (3) many possible outcomes following frustration or aversive experiences.

This model predicts that aversive experiences lead to emotional arousal and that the outcome of this state is governed by the anticipated consequences, which in turn depend on a history of reinforcement. Aggression would be most likely to occur under aversive circumstances to people who have been reinforced for the use of violence, either through role models or the successful achievement of desired goals.

There is empirical support for Bandura's social learning theory. In a review of theories of aggression, Megargee (1972) focuses on the question of how inhibitions to aggression are formed. For example, subjects in learning experiments gradually "warm up" to punishing the learner (Goldstein, Davis, & Herman, 1975). Their aggression becomes increasingly disinhibited when they are told to administer shock without aversive consequences.

People also learn violent behavior from role models. Families provide role models for violent behavior (Straus et al., 1980; Steinmetz, 1977; Steinmetz & Straus, 1973; Gelles, 1972). Families also provide the environment for learning that aggression and violence are effective ways of solving problems.

The family as an institution has unique structural conditions which affect the use of violence. Gelles and Straus (1979) assert that at least 12 aspects of the family are important to an explanation of intrafamily violence:

1. *Time at Risk.* The most elementary family characteristic accounting for the high incidence of violence is the fact that so many hours of the day are spent interacting with other family members. Although this is an important factor, the ratio of intrafamily violence to violence experienced outside the family far exceeds the ratio of time spent in the family to time spent outside the family. . . .

2. *Range of Activities and Interests.* . . . This means that there are more "events" over which a dispute or a failure to meet expectations can occur.

3. *Intensity of Involvement.* Not only is there a wider range of events over which a dispute or dissatisfaction can occur, but in addition, the degree of injury felt in such instances is likely to be much greater than if the same issue were to arise in relation to someone outside the family. . . .

4. *Impinging Activities.* Conflict is structured into such things as whether Bach or Mendelsshon will be played on the family stereo, whether to go to a movie or bowling, or a line-up for use of the bathroom.

5. *Right to Influence.* Membership in a family carries with it an implicit right to influence the behavior of others.

6. *Age and Sex Discrepancies.* The fact that the family is composed of people of different sexes and ages (especially during the child rearing years), coupled with the existence of generational and sex differences in culture and outlook on life, makes the family an arena of culture conflict.

7. *Ascribed Roles.* An aspect of this which has traditionally been a focus of contention is socially structured sexual inequality, or in contemporary language, the sexist organization of the family.

8. *Family Privacy.* In many societies the normative kinship, and household structure, insulates the family from both social controls and assistance in coping with intra-family conflict.

9. *Involuntary Membership.* There is first the social expectation of marriage as a long-term commitment, as expressed in the phrase "until death do us part." In addition, there are emotional, material, and legal rewards and constraints which frequently make membership in the family group inescapable, socially, physically, or legally.

10. *High Level of Stress.* . . . The nuclear family continuously undergoes changes in structure as a result of the birth of children, maturation of children, aging, and retirement. The crisis-like nature of these changes has long been recognized (LeMasters, 1957). All of this, combined with the huge emotional investment which is typical of family relationships, means that the family is likely to be the locus of more, and more serious, stresses than any other groups.

11. *Normative Approval.* Another aspect of the family which is important for understanding why so much violence occurs within that setting is the simple but important fact of *de jure* and *de facto* cultural norms legitimizing the use of violence between family members in situations which would make the use of physical force a serious moral or legal violation if it occurred between non family members.

12. *Socialization into Violence and Its Generalization.* It seems likely that an important part of the explanation for the high level of intrafamily violence lies in the fact that the family is the setting in which most people first experience physical violence, and also in the emotional context accompanying this experience.

The first of these unintended consequences is the association of love with violence. The child learns that those who love him or her the most are also those who hit and have the right to hit. The second unintended consequence is the lesson that when something is really important, it justifies the use of physical force. Finally, we suggest that these indirect lessons are not confined to providing a model for later treatment of one's own children. Rather, they become such a fundamental part of the individual's personality and world view that they are generalized to other social relationships, and especially to the relationship which is closest to that of parent and child: that of husband and wife. Therefore, it is suggested that early experience with physical punishment lays the groundwork for the normative legitimacy of all types of violence but especially intrafamily violence. (pp. 552–554)

Gelles and Straus (1979) contributes to the formulation of an explanation of intrafamily violence by isolating the aspects of families that lead to the family being a special case of violent behavior. Each of these authors separately and in collaboration with Steinmetz have also provided the soundest base of empirical findings about the incidence of intrafamily violence in the United States, and many empirically and theoretically relevant relationships between variables. (For a comprehensive report on those findings, see Straus *et al.*, 1980.)

Results of the study of family violence from a national sample survey of 2143 families indicate that "3.8% of the respondents reported one or more physical attacks which fall under our operational definition of wife beating. Applying this incidence rate to the approximately 47 million couples in the United States, means that in any one year, approximately 1.8 million wives are beaten by their husbands" (Straus, 1977a, p. 4).

The average number of violent attacks per year is eight and the median (the most typical number of attacks) is 2.4 for the subgroup of the sample that were violent. (Straus, 1977a). These figures are probably underestimates. Violence is regarded by many as so common and legitimate as to be unnoteworthy. Others are reluctant to talk about the violence because of shame or guilt. In addition the high incidence of violent acts associated with divorce has not been counted in these incidence rates because only intact couples were studied.

The level of wife beating in the United States is associated with four structural characteristics in the family: (1) the high level of violence in society which can carry over into the family, (2) the socialization in violence which occurs when parents use physical punishment on children and when parents use physical force on each other, (3) the cultural norms that legitimate the use of physical force and condone a man hitting his wife, and (4) the sexual inequality of society that is one of the most fundamental factors in all male–female relationships (Straus, 1977a).

Sexism, the use of violence to maintain power positions, cultural norms legitimizing violence, and the male-oriented organization of criminal justice systems are all related to patterns of wife battering (Straus, 1977a). Power is the common variable that underlies all of these conditions. Women in general have less power in society, and therefore less resources to prevent violence or to leave when violence occurs.

When both husband and wife—or either—have low power and status, for example, when the man is unemployed, rates of violence rise (Carlson, 1977; Straus et al., 1980). When the wives have a higher education level or higher status jobs, they seem to have increased risks of violence (Tidmarsh, 1976). If men are not in the positions of power they have come to expect as their role in society, they may use violence as a way to achieve power, especially power over their spouses. The greater the husband's resources, the less likely he is to use physical violence (Allen & Straus, 1975). In a study of 150 individuals filing for divorce, violence was more prevalent among families where the husband was unable to maintain a superior status position (O'Brien, 1971).

Sexual inequality in society is a primary factor in the battering of wives. The work of Del Martin (1976) and of Dobash and Dobash (1977) support these findings. Dobash and Dobash have been engaged in a comprehensive study of wife abuse since 1974. The first research year was spent studying police and court records to determine the extent of the problem and how the institutional structure has dealt with the problem. The second year they spent talking informally with battered women with the goal of developing an outline of the important issues and an interview schedule that covered the essential questions. A major problem for Dobash and Dobash was the attempt to combine the structural analysis of the problem of wife battering and the personal experiences of individually battered women. Their major contribution has come as a result of this struggle. Their work focuses on the important areas of the institutionalized ideologies concerning wife battering, and the interface between the institutions of social control and the women themselves. The major theme of their writings is that the patriarchal structure of society is dominated by a pattern of sub-servience for women that creates and perpetuates the problems of battered women. Dobash and Dobash (1977) state:

> "Love, honour and obey" is the lot of women in marriage. Care for him, look up to him and do as he wishes—or else. Implied in that vow is the threat of rightful control over those who fail to obey; control may take the form of coercion. Thus, foundations of wife battering are written into the marriage contract. The church as well as the state are complicitous in this.
>
> The struggle for battered women is not just a struggle for women who are beaten by their husbands or a struggle against the men who beat

their wives; it is a struggle against the structure and ideologies which support wife beating and the oppression of women in marriage. These ideologies have developed over a long period of time and have become so much a part of the culture that it took hundreds of years before wife beating was uncovered and defined as a social problem about which something should be done. (p. 403)

In summary, there is strong evidence that social structural factors such as socialization patterns, structural inequality in the class structure as evidenced in employment status, the relative position of women in society, and the general tolerance of violence—in particular, the tolerance of violence against women—are primary causal factors contributing to rates of wife beating.

How Does Wife Battering Occur in Relationships?

The question of "how" wife battering occurs rather than "why" reflects a different way of thinking about social behavior. This approach is based on the assumption that linear cause–effect analyses cannot capture the complexity of mutually causal relationships. The question of how violence develops over time to the level of wife battering, and how the wife battering becomes an ongoing pattern resistant to change requires a process approach.

As noted earlier, due to the structural features of families in our society, violence is more likely to occur within the family than between strangers. Both social structural variables and interpersonal–process variables influence how violence occurs (Goode, 1971). The family is a social system that is relatively well-defined by rules and structured power. The personal resources of each member of the system provide a basis for the processes of exchange within intimate relationships (Goode, 1971). For example, intimates exchange economic resources, status, and prestige, as well as qualities of attractiveness and personality characteristics. However, power within social systems ultimately depends on force or its threat, and the family social system is no exception (Goode, 1971). Men who lack sufficient resources to hold the socially prescribed dominant role in the family may use physical force to compensate for the lack of resources (Goode, 1971).

Rules within family systems define what behavior is acceptable and what is not acceptable within the system. Rule violations within family systems are often attributed to aggressiveness on the part of the rule violator (Hotaling, 1979). In addition, once an attribution of aggressiveness has been made, the subsequent expectation of aggressive behavior from that member tends to increase the probability of aggressive violence. Attribution theory demonstrates how interpersonal violence escalates. One incident of violence within a family system potentially changes the future pattern of interaction within the family. Once violence has occurred, the expectation of other family members that further violence will occur is increased, and this expectation itself tends to increase the likelihood of further violence.

These propositions are consistent with a general system's theory of family violence. Borrowing concepts from labeling theory to illustrate the processes that influence how violence occurs within family systems, Straus (1973) developed several propositions. Four are particularly relevant here.

First, violence occurs in most families, but the victims do not define themselves as victims at first, and the family system tends not to deal with the violence as a serious problem. "Most violence is either denied or not labeled as deviance" (Straus, 1973, p. 112).

Second, the victims may inadvertently be reinforcing the violent behavior. "Violent persons may be rewarded for violent acts if those acts produce the desired results" (Straus, 1973, p. 112). Patterson, Cobb, and Ray (1972) observed parents' reinforcement of the violence of their highly destructive boys. Just as the parents were not aware of reinforcements for such behavior, women in a battering relationship may not be aware of how they reinforce violent behavior. As a result, violence may become a stabilized pattern in the relationship.

Third, once violence has occurred, a rule against using violence has been broken, and this violation may precipitate further conflict increasing the likelihood of more violence. "Use of violence, when it is contrary to family norms, creates conflict over the use of violence to settle the original conflict" (Straus, 1973, p. 112).

Finally, as violence becomes known to others outside the family, the person labeled as violent may be encouraged to play out the role through the development of a self-concept as "violent." Using the same reasoning, the person labeled as victim may be encouraged to play out that role (Straus, 1973).

Following this same theoretical direction, Pagelow (1977) presents a process model of violence which includes three components. Model I explains the causative factor of woman battering, focusing primarily on the manifestation of traditional ideology in a broad range of internalized beliefs in acceptance of the "rightness" of the patriarchal–hierarchical order of the social structure. Model II explains the characteristics of the interacting male and female which determine if battering will occur. Model III explains systematic, repeated batterings as the result of processes within the system similar to the processes that have been outlined by Lemert (1967) to explain secondary deviance.

Both causative factors and process variables are used in this model to show how violence can become, over time, a patterned behavior, and also how the response of others in the family system can affect that pattern.

To explain processes that lead to secondary battering, Pagelow developed four theoretical propositions:

> 1. The greater the acceptance by the weaker partner of battering as a proper response to stress, and the more intense the traditional ideology, the greater the likelihood that battering will occur.
> 2. The greater the willingness to invest in conjugal relationships and the more intense the traditional ideology, the greater the likelihood that battering will not result in retaliation or termination of a conjugal relationship.
> 3. The more one partner responds to stressful situations by battering, the greater the willingness of the other to invest in conjugal relationships, and the more intense the traditional ideology of both, the more likely battering will occur.
> 4. The less likelihood there is of retaliation due to battering, the more likelihood there is that the batterer will continue, the longer the battering continues, the more frequently it occurs, and the greater its intensity.

Walker (1977-1978, 1979) makes two important contributions to the study of how wife battering occurs. The first is the description of a three-stage battering cycle, and the second is the application of the psychological concept of "learned helplessness" to the situation of battered women.

Walker's three-stage model consists of, first, the tense period of conflict escalation leading to the battering episode—the second stage—and then finally to a third stage of reconciliation marked by the man's contriteness and pleas for forgiveness and the woman's return to him. Walker maintains that this third stage provides the woman with the reinforcement to stay in the relationship.

The concept of "learned helplessness" helps explain how women stay for long periods of time in relationships in which they are being beaten (Walker, 1977-1978). Women learn that their voluntary attempts to change what is happening to them have no effect, thus over time the motivation to respond in an active way decreases. The subsequent passive behavior is due to a motivational deficit similar to that seen in rats whose reinforcement schedules have been arranged so that they never learn that they can control their environment through purposeful behavior.

Together these studies emphasize (1) exchange processes affect the likelihood of violence in family systems, (2) the attribution of aggression can lead to further escalation of conflict and violence, (3) the process of adaptation to violence over time is marked at first by denial, and later by labeling and escalation, (4) secondary battering as a pattern results from primary causative factors combined with the interaction processes between the man and the woman, and (5) the pattern of long-term battering is related to a cycle that reinforces staying for the woman, and also a process that decreases individual motivation of the woman to respond actively because she has learned that nothing she does will help her.

To further understand how wife-battering processes occur we must look at forces in the larger social system, and how they affect wife-battering patterns within families.

Forces That Lead to Stability in Patterns of Wife Battering

Processes of negative feedback within systems inhibit change and increase the likelihood of stability of established patterns. The definition of wife battering within the larger social system is one indication of the nature of feedback from the larger social system to different facets of the wife-battering process.

Tracing the rise of the movement for services for battered women, Dobash and Dobash (1977) found that one of the most serious obstacles was how the problem was defined. Wife battering is viewed as an individual problem and not as a problem within the structure of the family or of society. In contrast, advocates of women's rights view wife abuse as a form of institutionalized control that is sanctioned by the structure of society.

> Men may control their wives for many reasons. The most common ones are sexual jealousy—related to her status as property, and lack of compliance with his personal and household demands—related to her status as oppressed labourer. The agencies of the State, both legal and social, do not intervene in husbands' attempts to control their wives or they do so

ineffectively because the exploitation and oppression of women in the home serves the purposes of the State and the prevailing economic order. The structure of the system is such that women must be controlled. How better to achieve this than on a one-to-one basis in the privacy of the home? (Dobash & Dobash, 1977, p. 413)

Laws are now being changed to condemn rather than condone wife battering. Behavior that is governed by long-standing cultural norms, however, does not change as quickly as the writing on the pages of statute books. Wife battering continues to be implicitly condoned by at least some segments of the general public, the law enforcement and judicial officers (Field & Field, 1973; Dobash & Dobash, 1978; Straus, 1976).

The institutional supports of violence against women are deeply embedded in social processes, and there is a strong interrelationship between the institutions of law, economy, and government, as well as services such as the medical and therapeutic professions (Dobash & Dobash, 1978). A summary of findings from the research of Dobash & Dobash follows:

Regarding Nonreporting

Although very few women maintain a veil of complete silence throughout the years that they are beaten, most of them only report an infinitesimally small number of actual assaults they receive. For example, the 100 women we interviewed reported a total of approximately 32,000 assaults throughout their collective married lives, and yet only 517 of these assaults, about 2% were ever reported to the police. . . . Women do not report the violent treatment they are receiving because of factors which center on themselves, on their husbands and upon the agencies themselves. First, the woman's belief that the violence will cease makes outside help seem unnecessary and her own internalization of ideals of privacy, respectability, shame and guilt operate to inhibit reporting because of fear that she might be blamed or stigmatized. Second, the man's conceptions of privacy, respectability, shame and guilt prohibit him from seeking help for himself and he in turn prevents his wife from revealing the violence to others. Finally, the woman's willingness to approach others for help is affected by her initial perception of the ability and willingness of various individuals or agencies to give help, and later, by her experiences with them. (1979, pp. 3–4)

Regarding the Helping Professions

It is possible, for example, for an agency's policies to explicitly reject wife beating, and yet at the same time to actively support the type of marital relationship which reinforces the violence and forms the foundations of its continuation.

It is also possible for the policies of an agency to overtly reject any form of wife beating, and yet, for the particular practitioner involved to ignore, excuse or justify it when they have a case before them. The net results of either ignoring a beating or of excusing or justifying it are to merely set limits upon how far a man can actually go when hitting his wife and to specify the conditions under which he can get away with it. Underlying this Marquis of Queensbury [sic] approach to wife beating is a basic failure to clearly and unequivocally reject the idea that a man has a right to dominate and control his wife. (1979, p. 6)

Regarding the Medical Profession

In our own study we found that 75% of the women who went to the doctor received only treatment for their physical injuries although most of them had either eventually told their doctor about the source of the violence or suspected that he knew. Only 25% of these women ever discussed the beatings with the doctor and on such occasions he usually took a neutral or non-committal stance and just listened. Although advice was sometimes given, referrals were seldom made. (1979, p. 8)

Regarding the Prescription of Tranquilizers and Antidepressants

In our study, we did not specifically ask women if they had been given drugs, but 40% of the 87 women who went to the doctor spontaneously mentioned that they had received drugs. (1979, p. 12)

Regarding the Psychiatric Profession

Despite the rather widespread agreement among researchers in the field of family violence, including many psychiatrists, that men who beat their wives, like parents who beat their children cannot be usually characterized as pathological, there is a widespread "common sense" explanation that people who commit such acts, and sometimes even their victims, are by definition mentally ill, inadequate, deprived or in some way incomplete and that no explanation beyond these personal inadequacies need be sought. Underlying this belief in individual inadequacy or pathology is the implicit assumption that the legal, political, cultural, family and economic institutions in our society contribute little or nothing to the violence. (1979, p. 14–15)

Dobash and Dobash go on to review the psychiatric literature which emphasizes the mother–child relationship and the mother's responsibility for the creation of problems in the child which in turn become problems in the adult personality. This basic psychiatric perspective leads to the view that women are the cause of all violence, even that directed at them.

The diagnostic skills of professional helpers have been traditionally derived from Freudian psychoanalytic theory. The psychoanalytic perspective is not the only imagery brought to casework but because it reinforces conventional wisdom about the relationships between men and women it has compelling appeal. Elevated to the status of explanation, it identifies women as masochistic and/or provoking creatures who either seek or incite violence from men. (Dobash & Dobash, 1979, p. 27)

Even though one man may be violent to one woman, the institutionalized patterns of societal interaction inhibit change in systems. If women who are being battered do try to change the pattern by seeking help and receive negative feedback from professionals when they do, then little change will occur.

Police and social service agencies have often failed to respond adequately to battered women's search for help (Nichols, 1976; Parnas, 1977; Fields, 1976; Bard & Zacker, 1971). The policies of police and family agencies represent negative feedback.

This is a problem for battered women but also for the police (Bard & Zacker, 1971). There are constraints on police in crisis intervention programs that make the police relatively helpless to prevent impending violence. Forces that lead to stable patterns of violence both within individual families and within the larger social system do not originate from social service agencies. The service sector reflects, and is influenced by, the larger social structural conditions.

Stability in patterns of wife battering is maintained in part by the influence of the larger social system on individual families. The processes that go on within families are also causally linked to the processes within the larger social system. Families maintaining stable patterns of violence represent positive feedback to the larger social system processes. Neither the families nor the social system processes change under these conditions.

Forces That Lead to Change in Patterns of Wife Battering

Without new input into a system that has become stabilized in a pattern of wife battering, little change is likely to occur. Let us look, therefore, at sources of new input into the system. There are basically two sources of new input: (1) change in the larger social system, and (2) change in the boundaries of the family to include new information.

Inhibitions against violence and aggression are learned primarily through early family experiences. The early learning of children in the United States teaches that aggression is acceptable. If these early experiences of aggression, primarily from parents, are changed, this would represent new input from the larger social system about the acceptability of using violence in loving relationships.

Change can occur over time in learned patterns of behavior if the reinforcement schedule also changes. For example, there is evidence that aggression can be reduced through sanctions (Bandura, 1973). Sanctions can take the form of legal restrictions or of informal norm enforcement.

The absence of sanctions for wife abuse inhibits change. If the social structure accepts wife abuse as normal or at least tolerable (Straus, 1977a; Dobash & Dobash, 1977; Martin, 1976), change has to come from groups that oppose the normative structure. The women's movement has provided the ideological basis and the power that comes from collective effort to oppose the normative acceptance of wife battering.

Groups associated with the women's movement and some social service agencies have opened an increasing number of shelters in the United States. Whereas in 1973 there were fewer than five shelters in this country, there are now at least 300 programs to provide services for battered women.

The movement for women's shelters encourages change in battering patterns by providing an alternative source of shelter and support for women. In the past women have had few places to go and few resources to aid them in their flight. Shelters provide at least temporary protection, as well as an interim place to live for a period of time in which the women may be able to make further changes in their lives. They may either be able to renegotiate their relationships with the men, or they may decide to leave the relationships.

Shelters, however, represent only a temporary solution to the problem of wife battering. Changes in the larger social system need to become more widespread before significant change will occur in the extent of wife battering (Bell, 1977; Gelles, 1977b; Marcovitch, 1976). These broader changes of scope include legal status, police training, social attitudes toward violence, and improvement in the status of women in society.

Being in a state of "learned helplessness" deprives women of the motivation to change their own situation (Walker, 1977–1978). This lack of motivation is the result of having no available sources of help when women have sought aid.

The increasing availability of services, support groups, and shelters raises several interesting questions about the impact of this new input within systems characterized by wife-battering processes. Outside help theoretically provides new input into the family system that may change established patterns.

The change within systems in response to new input may lead to negative or positive consequences. Change that brings the violence to the attention of others, and provides support for the woman, may in fact increase the violence at least in the short run.

Long-run changes require more fundamental change in the larger social system. Changes that sanction violence represent positive feedback to a search for help outside the family system. Positive feedback tends to increase the likelihood that the behavior (seeking help in this case) will occur again. This feedback to new behavior theoretically will change the patterns of interaction that have become stabilized within the system. The nature of that change is a question open to empirical investigation.

CHAPTER 3

A Profile of the Characteristics and Relationships of the 31 Women

Thirty-one women who were part of ongoing violent relationships participated in this study. They do not in any way represent all battered women, or even all women who have sought help at a shelter. Their experiences provide insight, however, into the process of battering relationships. The histories of their violent relationships let us observe as directly as possible the experiences of a violent relationship, and the impact of that violence on the individual woman.

All of these women were interviewed when they first came to a shelter, and 24 were reinterviewed four to six months after their stay at the shelter. The first interviews ranged from one to three hours, and the follow-up interviews ranged from two to six hours. Three women were asked in addition to allow me to tape-record their account of the violent relationship. With both types of interviews, I put together both a quantitative sketch or the women's relationships over time, and a qualitative presentation of the life histories of three women: Debbie, Elizabeth, and Paula. First, let me describe all of these women and some salient characteristics of their relationships.

WHO ARE THEY?

The women in this study represented a range of demographic backgrounds (see Table 3-1). There are, however, some marital characteristics that may be related to their violent histories.

TABLE 3-1. Demographic characteristics of the women and their partners

Marital status	
Married	61%
Cohabiting	26%
Separated	6.5%
Divorced	6.5%
Length of relationship	
Range	4 months to 29 years
Mean	5.7 years
Five years or less	68%
Number of relationship for women	
First	55%
Second	35%
Third	10%
Number of relationship for men	
First	45%
Second	35%
Third	20%
Children from prior relationships	
Women	35%
Men	46%
Number of children for women	
Range	0 to 7
Mean	2.5
No children	6%
Age of women	
Range	18 to 47 years
Mean	29.1 years
Age of men	
Range	19 to 48 years
Mean	32.7 years
Age differences	
Women older (7)	
Range	1 to 11 years
Men older (24)	
Range	1 to 22 years

The number of women and men who were in cohabiting relationships is unusually high. During the sexual revolution and the general loosening of constraints on people living openly together, cohabiting was viewed as an innovation that would increase the equality between the pair. In turn, greater equality has been associated with better personal relationships. But who benefits in a living together relationship, and what kinds of conflicts may arise? These questions are central to an understanding of violence in cohabiting relationships. In at least one other study cohabiting couples had violence rates as much as twice as high as did married couples (Yllo & Straus, 1980).

TABLE 3-1. (Continued)

Racial/ethnic background	
Anglo-American	94%
Oriental	3%
American Indian	3%
Religion	
Protestant	58%
Catholic	29%
Other	13%
Education of women	
Eight years or less	6%
Some high school	23%
High school graduate	39%
Some college or special training	28%
Unknown	3%
Education of men	
Eight years or less	16%
Some high school	32%
High school graduate	26%
Some college or special training	22%
Unknown	3%
Employment of women (35% employed)	
Technical managerial	16%
Skilled worker	16%
Unskilled worker	60%
Student	8%
Employment of men (65% employed)	
Professional	3%
Technical managerial	13%
Skilled worker	33%
Unskilled worker	43%
Student	3%
Unknown	3%
Unemployment history of men	
Once during relationship	19%
A few times	3%
Several times	6%
Many times	29%

Many of these women were in remarried relationships or living together after divorce. A few of the women spontaneously told me that their prior relationship had been violent as well, but the more common revelation was that the man had also been violent with a prior woman. Some people may go from one violent relationship to another, as Elizabeth's story in Chapter 5 reveals, but there may also be some particular problems in remarried relationships that increase the chance of violence.

These women also tend to vary from the norm in the range of differences in age between themselves and their partners. These specific characteristics raise such questions as this. Does violence become more common in relationships that are outside the normative expectations for American marriages? Unfortunately, such questions can only be answered with further investigation of other groups.

The women in this study and their partners are predominantly blue-collar or lower class, with over half their incomes falling below the $10,000 level as indicated in Table 3-2. Women and partners with different socioeconomic backgrounds are not compared in this study. Some controversy exists, however, about whether or not wife battering is predominantly a blue-collar to lower-class phenomenon. Violence rates were found to be higher in a national survey among blue-collar and lower classes, but not to the degree that had been suspected (Straus *et al.*, 1980). The myth, if it is one, that poorer people fight more than the affluent continues to be prevalent because of stereotyped representations of battered women, and because poorer people in general are more exposed to public scrutiny. In addition, working- and lower-class families have higher rates of use of community public agencies, thus more public information becomes available. Middle- and upper-class people tend to use private physicians, whose records are sealed.

The relatively low income and the high unemployment of the women in this study and their partners is important in itself. Low income or unemployment may produce problems that lead to violence. On the other hand, not all people who lose their jobs or who have low incomes engage in violent acts. The income and employment problems alone do not explain violence. No demographic characteristics alone can provide the answers, but in combination with other social char-

TABLE 3-2. Percentage of women and men by income

INCOME	WOMEN	MEN
0	23%	3%
Less than $1000	16%	3%
$1000–2499	10%	6%
$2500–3999	16%	3%
$4000–5999	19%	19%
$6000–7999	13%	13%
$8000–9999	3%	10%
$10,000–11,999		3%
$12,000–14,999		19%
$15,000–19,999		6%
$20,000–24,999		3%
Don't know		10%

TABLE 3-3. Percentage of women and men by experience of violence as children

EXPERIENCE OF VIOLENCE[a]	WOMEN ($n = 31$)	MEN ($n = 31$)
Observed parental violence	19%	23%
Reported beatings beyond "normal" spankings	29%	48%
No violence reported	52%	19%
Don't know	3%	19%

[a]This was asked as an open-ended question, and answers were coded. Some cases were recorded both as "observed" and as being beaten.

acteristics and information about the process of the violent relationship, some understanding is possible.

Early experiences of violence, in particular, contribute to the learning of violence as an appropriate way to act with other people in families, with people one loves, and with those who may frustrate one most personally. Intimacy in families is a patterned activity, and ways to act in intimate relationships are learned as other behavior is learned. It is no surprise then to find that people who either observed violence between their parents or experienced violence as a child are many more times as likely to hit and abuse both children and spouses (Straus *et al.*, 1980). The women in this study and their partners are examples of this intergenerational linkage in violent activity. As Table 3-3 indicates, many women in this study reported that they and/or their partners experienced violence as children. Almost half of the women and almost three-quarters of the men had either observed their parents fighting or been beaten themselves. This information comes only from the women; however, the reports probably accurately reflect the women's experiences and underestimate the men's early experiences. If the men had told the women about violence they experienced as children, women are not likely to misrepresent that, but some may not know if there had been violence in the men's backgrounds, because they had not been told.

The learned patterns of violence again, however, do not explain violent behavior between the women and their partners. Some people who have experienced violence as children will never be violent themselves. To further understand the factors that may be presented in combination to produce violence, it is important to know what problems the women reported.

Alcohol or alcoholism has been considered a cause of wife battering, or at least a common concurrent phenomenon (see Coleman &

Straus, 1979, for a complete discussion of this issue). When I asked the women to look at a list of problems people may have in marriage, and tell me if they had that problem, alcohol did stand out as one of the most significant problems reported in addition to the violence. As Table 3-4 indicates, however, alcohol is one of many problems they reported. Money, jealousy, children, sex, household tasks, and the woman's income or employment were all frequently reported as problems. The picture that emerges from this is of multiproblem marriages, and it is not possible from this material to know whether alcohol may have caused other problems, or even whether other problems may have caused the alcohol problem. Alcohol was, however, the problem reported by the largest percentage of the women as their most serious problem.

I asked about the amount of alcohol used, the length of time alcohol had been used, and the ability to go for long periods of time without alcohol. These are not accepted indicators to discriminate between alcoholics and other categories of drinkers, but on the basis of this informal questioning, I estimated that 6% of the women in this study and 35% of their partners could be considered alcoholics. I do not have complete information on the presence or absence of alcohol for specific incidents of violence, but informally even those considered alcoholic were violent at times when they had not been drinking, as well as when they had been drinking. Wives of probable alcoholics did consider the alcohol to be related to the violence, however.

Alcohol does not necessarily lead to violence, just as other problems do not necessarily lead to violence. In fact, the presence of violence is

TABLE 3-4. Percentage citing presence of problem and percentage citing each problem as most serious (n = 31)

LIST OF PROBLEMS	CITING PRESENCE	MOST SERIOUS
Arguments over money	86%	0%
Man jealous	90%	7%
Woman jealous	55%	7%
Man's use of alcohol or drugs	72%	38%
Woman's use of alcohol or drugs	10%	
Things about the children	90%	21%
Sex and affection	83%	7%
Household tasks	76%	
Pregnancy or birth control	24%	
Man's income or employment	59%	
Woman's income or employment	69%	
Other	79%	21%

quite likely to lead to problems in other areas—for example, sex and affection—or to the reinterpretation of some aspect of the other's behavior as problematic.

Given all of these problems and a history of violence, it is not surprising that most of these women were very unhappy with their marriages when they first came to the shelter. But despite being very unhappy, many women felt that their marriages were not all bad. Despite the violence, most women told about good times they had had with the men, or admitted that the men had some good qualities. This ambivalence shows up in the number of women who leave shelters and go back to the men who have beaten them. This ambivalence is not unique to violent relationships, however. Divorce or separation produces mixed feelings of relief, regret over the loss of attachments, and insecurity about the future, which often lead to at least attempts at reconciliation.

The pattern of male dominance prevalent in our society has also been associated with patterns of violence. There is some controversy, however, about whether the idea that men have "rights" over their wives serves to rationalize violence (Dobash & Dobash, 1977), or whether the threat or use of force serves as an "ultimate resource" men have to induce women to grant them more power (Allen & Straus, 1979; Goode, 1971). If we take a general systems theory approach, the two ideas do not compete. Both the rationalizing of violence as legitimate and the attempt to get more power through violence are interdependent patterns in the overall system of ongoing behavior.

The women in this study reported interesting patterns of marital power. They indicated that over half of the couples (52%) were male-dominated, but a significant minority (13%) were female-dominated. Compared with Blood and Wolfe's (1960) findings that 25% of American marriages were husband-dominant and only 3% wife-dominant, it appears that most of these relationships are from the extreme ends of the expected norm.

The majority of women were living in households that were dominated almost entirely by the men. It is impossible to know whether the men in these cases felt that beating their wives or living partners was their "right." Some women had been told just that, however. Thus was true in Paula's case, for example, as can be seen in Chapter 6.

The number of problems reported by the women and the unusual number of wife-dominant marriages may also lend support to the "ultimate resource theory." The violence may have been a way of gaining power. There were a high number of unemployed men, and of lower-class men who did not have other sources of legitimate power in society. These problems may contribute to the need to assert power over women.

In some cases the women provided the only income the couple received, either through working, through A.D.C. checks, or through a combination of the two. This may account for the relatively high number of wife-dominant marriages. Because of their resources, and because they were able to leave the man without loss of income, they may have gained more power in the relationship than would be expected.

Even though the women's dominance stands out as unusual, it represents only a small minority of the cases. The most striking fact is still that over half of these women felt that what happened to them was most often determined by the men. On the whole they felt powerless, and often depressed.

Most of the women said that their experiences and depression isolated them from other people for significant periods of time. Some were very isolated when they first came to the shelter, but almost three-fourths (71%) indicated that they did have someone to talk to when they felt low or depressed. Family violence is often a hidden problem. Abused wives and abused children are often literally hidden from outside view, because they stay or are kept at home. It is not uncommon to hear either "He wouldn't even let me go to the store," or "I was too ashamed to show my face." It was, therefore, an important discovery to find that so many of these women reported they did have people to talk to about what had happened. When I asked how long they had been close to that other person, a majority indicated a year or less. Many women spontaneously mentioned that this person also had been beaten, or that the person had helped them leave the relationship. The presence of a confidante provides support during crises, and may ease the problems of adaptation to major life changes (Lowenthal & Haven, 1968). In these cases, the presence of a confidante turned out to be the major factor in the attempt to leave the battering relationship. This will be discussed later as a bridging relationship.

PATTERNS OF VIOLENCE

All of the women in this study had experienced violence, and several questions arise about those patterns of violence. How violent were both the women and their partners? What kinds of violence did they use and endure? Were the patterns of violence reciprocal between the women and the men? What happened to these battered women after they left the temporary shelter?

First, let us look at the extent of the different types of violence that the women and their partners used. The questions asked of each respondent were, "I'm going to read a list of some things that you and your partner might have done when you had a dispute, and I would first like you to tell me for each one how often you did it in the past year, and how often your partner did it in the past year." (See Appendix A for a complete discussion of the Conflict Tactics Scales.) These questions were asked of the women when they first came to the shelter and again six months after their stay.

Table 3-5 compares the percentage of men and women in the study who reported each violent act at least once in the 12 months prior to coming to the shelter (time 1) and in the 6 months after they came to the shelter (time 2). The Violence Index and the Abuse Index represent the percentage who had used any of the tactics in the items indicated.

TABLE 3-5. Comparison of the percentage of men and women who reportedly used each violent act at least once at time 1 and time 2

	MEN		WOMEN	
CONFLICT TACTICS SCALES VIOLENCE ITEM	TIME 1 ($n = 30$)	TIME 2 ($n = 24$)	TIME 1 ($n = 31$)	TIME 2 ($n = 24$)
Violence Index (K to R)	100.0	50.0	77.4	41.7
Abuse Index (N to R)	96.8	33.3	58.1	16.7
K. Threw something at spouse	80.6	12.5	35.5	12.5
L. Pushed, grabbed, shoved spouse	96.8	41.7	51.6	12.5
M. Slapped spouse	90.3	25.0	42.2	33.3
N. Kicked, bit, or hit with fist	77.4	25.0	35.5	12.5
O. Hit or tried to hit with something	67.7	20.8	41.9	4.2
P. Beat up spouse	83.9	29.2	12.9	8.3
Q. Threatened with a knife or gun	54.8	4.2	29.0	0.0
R. Used a knife or gun	25.0	0.0	16.7	0.0

Note. In this table the percentage of those who were violent in the 12 months before the stay at the shelter at least once are compared to the percentage of the follow-up sample who were violent at least once. Of course, some who were never violent in the 6 months following the stay at the shelter may have used violence in the subsequent 6 months. Those data are not available. However, I suspect most of the men and women studied who would use violence in a year would have used violence in the 6-month period. These figures are compared on the basis of that assumption with the necessary qualifications.

A high percentage of both the men and women used violence in the year before the women came to the shelter. The men had almost all abused the women seriously enough to cause injury. In many cases the beatings had been life threatening. Over half of the women had been threatened with a knife or gun, and one-fourth had been assaulted with a knife or gun.

Some of the women also had been violent in the year before they came to the shelter. Over half had acted in ways that could cause serious injury to the man. Unfortunately, we cannot compare the extent of injury to each of the people involved in these relationships because the men were not interviewed. Many of the women did receive serious injuries ranging from bruises to skull fractures and facial slashes, however. None of the women reported injuries that men received. Both men and women use violent tactics in these relationships. The considerable average weight difference between the sexes works to the disadvantage of women, thus, despite similar reported acts, it is more common for women to suffer injury.

A comparison of the levels of violence reported by the women for themselves and for their partners indicates that on most items almost twice as many men used each violent tactic as did the women. Why did some women engage in violence and others did not? Many women told me that they "just couldn't" or that if they did, they would get hit harder. In a minority of the cases, the patterns of violence were reciprocal. But the more common pattern was for the violence to be primarily one-sided, even in the case of some of the most severely beaten women. Not responding and trying not to feel or react was one adaptation to being beaten. Why some women are violent and what difference in outcomes result from reciprocal violence as opposed to one-sided violence is an issue which has never been thoroughly explored.

The case studies presented in the next three chapters provide at least some insight on this issue. Paula and Debbie both reported they had been violent at least once, although neither of them used violence frequently. Elizabeth never hit back, and this becomes quite important in her story.

Comparing the percentage of both men and women (as reported by the women) for the two time intervals (see Table 3-5) indicates that fewer men and women were violent in the six months after the stay at the shelter than in the year prior to the stay. The greatest difference appears in the most serious acts of violence—beating up the spouse, threatening with a knife or gun, and using a knife or gun. In the six-month follow-up period about 30% of the women were beaten up by their men. This is a reduction from almost 90% reported in the year prior to the stay at the shelter. The use of a knife or gun dropped to zero and threatening with a knife or gun by the men dropped to only 1%.

These reductions are dramatic. The change over time has improved the situation for most of these women. But, not for all. From the perspective that everybody has the right not to be beaten, we can see that many women are still victimized. This was the case whether they were living with the men after their stay at the shelter or not. In one very dramatic case, a young woman in this study got her own apartment only to find that she could not escape the violence. The man found out where she lived, broke into the apartment, beat her, and raped her. It is not uncommon for men to pursue women who try to move out of battering relationships. All three of the case studies that follow illustrate this.

Women were also less violent in the follow-up period than prior to coming to the shelter. The reduction is not as dramatic as that for men, because the original percentages were approximately half of the male percentages.

In both cases of change over time, we cannot automatically assume that the change over time was due to the intervening stay at the shelter. Several other factors intervened that may have caused change. Examples of other factors that may account for change are age, changes in residence, changes in societal norms, or other changes in the people themselves (Campbell & Stanley, 1966). Of these, the most intuitively reasonable factors that could account for the change are change of residence and change in the people themselves. The shelter programs were designed to facilitate both of these changes if the women expressed the desire to do so.

Table 3-6 reports the average number of times the women indicated that both men and women used each type of violent tactic in the year preceding the stay at the shelter and in the six-month follow-up period. Each of the women answered the question "How often did you and your partner do each of these things?" The number of times each act was reported could range from zero to "more than 20 times" (see Appendix A for details on the Conflict Tactics Scales). The average number of times different violent acts occurred underestimates the number of times the women in this study were subjected to each of these acts. The category "more than 20 times" includes all the cases in which violence occurred weekly or even more often. Thus, average number of times in each time period is based in many cases on gross underestimates.

Women were slapped, kicked, beaten up, threatened, and so forth, many times before they came to the shelter. The range of times beatings had occurred was from once to almost daily. Only one woman came to the shelter after being beaten once. For all others, the beatings had become regular patterned occurrences.

As shown earlier all men acted violently at least once, and in addition about three-fourths of the women did at some point. The difference between men's and women's violent behavior comes into sharper focus by looking at only those who were violent and seeing how often on the average they resorted to violent tactics. Women reported that almost all violent tactics were used by men twice as often, and in many cases several times more often than by women. I want to again remind readers that many women were never violent, and the averages of occurrence in Table 3-6 are based only on those who were violent as indicated by the n's.

The same scales of violent acts were used in a national random sample of American families (Straus et al., 1980). When results from the present study are compared to the results from the national sample, both the women in this study and their partners were more likely to use violence than would be expected by "normal" rates of violence. The women in this study also reported that they and their partners used violence more frequently than those from the national sample. The rates for men differ between the two study groups much more than the rates for women do, however. The women in this study who are violent do not abuse their partners any more than the violent women in the national sample did on the average. On the other hand, the women in this study reported that the men abused them much more frequently than men in the national sample did on the average.

Comparing the two time periods (the year prior to the women coming to the shelter and the six months after) indicates that the average number of times violence occurred was dramatically reduced in the six months after the initial interview. This reduction in frequency is among those who were violent, and we have already discussed the reduction in the number of men and women who were violent between the two periods. The women did not show the same reduction in frequency of violent acts if they were ever violent, as the men did. Because the two time periods are not equal intervals, the frequencies

TABLE 3-6. Comparison of mean number[a] of violent acts for men and women reported at time 1 and time 2[b]

CONFLICT TACTICS SCALES VIOLENCE ITEM	MEN		WOMEN	
	TIME 1 ($n = 31$)	TIME 2 ($n = 12$)	TIME 1 ($n = 24$)	TIME 2 ($n = 8$)
Violence Index (K to R)	68.7	4.83	19.25	3.6
Abuse Index (N to R)	32.2	2.62	9.85	3.0
K. Threw something at spouse	10.1	2.30	2.70	2.0
L. Pushed, grabbed, shoved spouse	10.1	1.80	6.40	3.3
M. Slapped spouse	13.6	1.30	5.70	2.1
N. Kicked, bit, or hit with fist	11.4	1.30	9.70	1.0
O. Hit or tried to hit with something	8.4	1.60	4.40	8.0[c]
P. Beat up spouse	9.8	1.30	6.25	1.0
Q. Threatened with a knife or gun	10.7	1.00	1.80	0.0
R. Used a knife or gun	3.5	0.00	1.20	0.0

[a]Mean of those engaged in each act. Omits those with zero scores.
[b]The two time periods reported here are not equal. For a more specific comparison, each of these figures could be divided by 12 (for time 1) or 6 (for time 2) to get a rate per month. This was not done because the numbers are so small in some cases.
n = 1.

during the six-month time period cannot be reported as a ratio to the earlier time period. We must look at them separately. But, the men who were violent in the six months following the initial interview had a dramatically smaller mean number of violent acts than violent men did in the prior period. The violent women had lower mean numbers of violent acts, but the difference is not as dramatic as for the men.

As mentioned earlier, these changes over time are not attributable totally to the intervening stay at the shelter. Age, changes in living arrangements, and other changes in the women may account for some reduction.

Again, I want to emphasize that many women were never violent at all. Even in the six-month follow-up period the number of women who were never violent is much lower than the number of men who were never violent. In addition, physical differences in size and strength make the impact of these violent acts different for men than for women. When we look at the impact of the acts rather than the acts alone, the women's victimization stands out. The women in the study suffered severe violence at the hands of their partners, many to the point of serious injury or attempts on their lives. For most, this occurred many times, and an escape often seemed hopeless.

CIRCUMSTANCES SURROUNDING
THREE VIOLENT INCIDENTS

A systems theory approach alerts us to the importance of any changes in ongoing patterns of activity. A variation in established patterns requires a new response from other members of the system. For example, in the case of a couple system, a new event such as the birth of a child requires new responses if the system is to continue.

When violence has occurred, the specific circumstances around that violence are critical to understanding how patterns become established. New demands or stressful situations commonly occur in marriages. Several questions arise about how couples cope with new demands. Is violence a response to stress? Is it perhaps an attempt to reestablish an equilibrium in the system? What are the rules concerning violent behaviors? How does the victim respond when violence first occurs? How might this response affect the use of violence in the future? To help define the situation, the women in this study answered a series of questions about each of three incidents of violence: (1) the very first incident, (2) one incident that stood out in their minds as important, and (3) the most recent incident.

Topics discussed in this section will include: (1) status of the relationship at the time, (2) preceding incidents or stressful situations, (3) whether the women felt guilty about what happened, (4) whether the women were angry at themselves, (5) whether the women felt angry at their partners, (6) whether the women were willing to "forgive and forget" at the time, (7) whether the women thought at the time the violence was a pattern or an isolated incident, (8) attributions of responsibility for each incident, and (9) whether there was any intervention at the time.

The results of questions on these topics are presented in Table 3-7 for each of the three incidents. The topics will be discussed separately, emphasizing the change over the three incidents.

Marital Status at Time of Incident

When the first violent incident occurred, 13% of the women were neither married to, nor living with, the man. In each case, however, they later made that move. This indicates that for these women, one incident of violence did not scare them off. In addition, 10% of those who were living together when the first incidents occurred later married the man.

In all, a minimum of 23% of the women increased their commitment to the man *after* the first incident.

Is the marriage license a "hitting license" (Straus, 1977a, p. 455)? Although a majority of the women in this study experienced violence only after marriage, many men hit the women earlier in the relationship. The acceptance of violence in marriage reflects larger social system rules legitimatizing violence toward others and particularly toward women. Violence occurs in male–female interaction across all different living arrangements. The marriage contract may strengthen that pattern, but the larger society's rules about rights of men and women provide the ultimate legitimatization.

Over the three incidents there was a small increase in the percentage who were married. There was also an increase in the percentage who were separated and divorced. This provides an indicator that separation and divorce do not protect the woman from violence.

Preceding Events or Stressful Situations

The events or stressful situations which occurred just prior to the violent incidents are important, because variation triggers new responses to regulate the ongoing system. The number of stressful events reported decreases over time. Since people could indicate more than one event, this is difficult to see from Table 3-7, but a total of 161 events were listed for the first incident, 99 for the second, and 95 for the third. This suggests that stress may be more important for precipitating the first incidents, but may not be necessary to precipitate a second incident. Once violence occurs, it may be easier for it to occur again. If the other member of the couple system responds with violent acts when stress is introduced into the system, and that violence meets the goals of reestablishing equilibrium in the system, then it is more likely to occur again given the same or similar events.

For the first incident, the most frequently cited stress category was a move. A move could be simply to a new apartment or to a different town or state. A high incidence of moves reported here is probably related to the fact that in most cases the first incidents of violence occurred shortly after the man and woman moved in together or were married. The second most frequent category cited is a pregnancy or birth of a child. Again, this may be related to the stage of marriage, because many of the women were pregnant when they were married. Gelles (1977a) and Van Stolk (1976) found that pregnant women were

TABLE 3-7. Circumstances surrounding each of three incidents of violence

TOPIC	AT FIRST INCIDENT (%)	AT IMPORTANT INCIDENT (%)	AT MOST RECENT INCIDENT (%)
Marital status			
Single	13	0	0
Living together	35	27	21
Married	48	58	58
Separated or divorced	3	16	19
Preceding events or stressful situations			
Loss of job by man	10	16	17
New job of woman	13	13	3
Pregnancy or birth	32	16	0
Illness in family	13	10	7
Problems with children	0	3	7
Problems with extended family	10	3	10
Move	39	16	7
Woman making new friends	6	6	17
Man making new friends	3	0	0
Recent separation or divorce of one from another partner	19	0	0
Business or job stress	0	3	10
Reconciliation	0	0	3
None	0	16	24
Women's guilt (% "yes")	41	22	26
Women angry at selves (% "yes")	32	24	21

particularly vulnerable to abuse. Gelles outlines five major factors that may be responsible for violence during pregnancy: (1) the sexual frustration of the man, (2) the impact of the family transition and the associated stress and strain, (3) the biochemical changes in the wife, (4) prenatal child abuse, and (5) the defenselessness and dependency of the wife. Each of these factors represents a variation in the ongoing couple system. The birth of a child alters the number of persons in the system, the patterns of interaction, and the amount of time and energy available to any one member of the system.

The third most frequently cited preceding situation was the recent separation or divorce of either the man or the woman from another partner. Separations and divorces are inherently stressful life changes that bring additional stress to the new relationship. In addition, the previous partner often makes demands on, or in other ways frustrates the person trying to make a new relationship.

TABLE 3-7. (Continued)

TOPIC	AT FIRST INCIDENT (%)	AT IMPORTANT INCIDENT (%)	AT MOST RECENT INCIDENT (%)
Women angry at partner (% "yes")	86	92	90
Willing to "forgive and forget" (% "yes")	93	29	18
Part of pattern or isolated violence			
Isolated incident	90	0	0
Part of pattern	10	100	100
Attributions of responsibility			
Self—behaviorally	16	10	10
Self—characterologically	3	0	7
Partner—behaviorally	16	17	14
Partner—characterologically	45	55	55
Both	6	14	3
Outside stress—external	10	3	7
Intervention			
Informal social control (family, friends, counselors, or medical help)	13	30	55
Formal social control (police or lawyers)	23	20	35
Leaving house for longer than brief period of time	3	10	58
No intervention	64	40	3

Preceding events for the second incident show fewer high frequencies for any category. Loss of a job by the husband, pregnancy or birth, a move, a woman wanting to leave the relationship, and the category "none" were all reported by 16% of the women. Loss of a job by the husband may precipitate financial problems, a loss of status, loss of self-esteem by the man, and a loss of respect from the woman. All of these may increase conflict and possibly violence. Pregnancy again appears for several couples. The woman wanting to leave the relationship preceded the violent incident in 14 to 16% of the couples for each of the three incidents. If a woman makes her intention to leave known, violence, coercive attempts to keep her in the relationship, and/or attempts to punish her may follow.

No stressful events preceded the second incident for 16% of the women and for 24% of the women at the third incident. Over time more women could think of no preceding events or stressful situations associated with the violent incident. Over time, the violence may become a patterned way of relating in the system rather than a behavioral response to stress and frustration.

Women's Guilt

Do women feel guilty about their abuse? In this sample, women felt less guilty about what had happened than expected, based on other studies (Martin, 1976; Gelles, 1976; Walker, 1979). Forty-one percent felt guilt at the time of the first incident, 22% at the second, and 26% at the third. In addition, the guilt they did experience relates to specific things they did. For example, going out with another man was mentioned as the reason precipitating guilt after the first incident in one case. Other reasons for guilt included guilt for staying so long, especially when children were being harmed, and also guilt for leaving when they finally did. Guilt for the actual violence concerned few women.

The women's guilt declines over the three incidents. Women less often define their behavior as at fault over a period of time and thus feel less guilty.

Women's Anger at Themselves

Women's anger at themselves did not change significantly over the three incidents. Less than a third of the women felt some anger at themselves at the time of the incidents.

The reasons for the women's anger was not systematically recorded, but informal mention indicated the reasons varied from legitimate anger for some precipitating incident to anger that they were in the situation at all—that they had not left it before.

Women's Anger at Man

Approximately 90% of the women were angry at the man for the violence, and again this does not change significantly over time. I asked this question directly, because so often women hide anger. When I looked at what the women did following these incidents, I found that often, although they felt anger, they did not act in angry, retaliatory ways. The number of women who sought help or intervention increased over the three incidents.

One can interpret this in two ways. First, women become more capable of exercising options when angry or victimized. Second, the violence becomes more severe, less easily denied, and women in desperation seek outside help.

Willing to "Forgive and Forget"

Do battered women forgive the man after beatings and forget what happened? "Yes" responses to this question declined sharply over the three incidents (from 93% to 29% to 18%). Almost all the women accepted and forgave one incident, but by the time a pattern had become established, less than a third were willing to forgive and forget. By the final incident, less than one-fifth were willing to do so. The fact that almost 20% were still willing to forgive and forget may be the surprising revelation of these figures.

Pattern of Violence or Isolated Incident

When did women recognize the violence as a pattern? Most women thought the first violent incident was an isolated incident that probably would not happen again. Only three women thought the violence was a pattern after only one incident. One woman said she took violence for granted. In her words, "Violence to me was like getting up and brushing your teeth. It would happen every day, all day." This woman had been severely physically and sexually abused by her father and also by a man in a relationship prior to the present one. Another woman who said it was a pattern after the first incident also was abused as a child and in a prior relationship. The third woman had not been abused as a child, but she firmly believed that hitting was "like eating one chip—once you start, you can't stop."

Over the three incidents, the women changed their assessment almost totally. By the second or "particularly important" incident (which was not the second that occurred) almost all the women realized the violence was part of a pattern. None thought it would never happen again. The women reported the third incident exactly the same way. Some time before the women left the relationship they were sure violence was an ongoing pattern that probably would not change. This contradicts some of Walker's (1979) findings that after each incident the man becomes contrite and remorseful and convinces the woman it will never happen again.

Attributions of Responsibility

The answers to the question "Who or what do you think was responsible for this happening?" were recorded verbatim. They were later coded using an attribution theory framework that had been used in a study of rape victims (Janoff-Bulman, 1978). Overall, the women thought the man was resonsible for what happened, and across the three incidents this tendency increased. When they held themselves responsible, they mentioned some aspect of their behavior that was responsible for the incident happening, rather than some aspect of their characterological makeup—that is, personality or character.

On the other hand, when they held the partner responsible, they mentioned some aspect of his character or personality that was responsible for the incident happening, more often than some aspect of his behavior. An example of this was when a woman said it happened because "he is sick" rather than "he just came in and belted me."

It is quite possible that the attributions of responsibility to the man—especially characterological responsibility—for the violent incidents result from attempts to rationalize their leaving by blaming the man for all of the violence. To guard against this problem, I asked very specifically who they had thought was responsible for the violence at the time it had happened. Reconstructing incidents detail by detail reduces the possibility of general negative evaluation being reported for each incident.

Intervention

When do women seek outside intervention? Who do they go to for help? After the first incident, 64% of the women reported they sought no intervention. This decreased dramatically over time to 40% after the second incident and to only 3% after the last incident. It is interesting to see what kind of intervention the women report most frequently. For the first incident, 23% called the police or sought a lawyer to get some formal social control. Thirteen percent went to friends, family, counselors, or medical help, and 3% left the house for longer than brief periods of time.

Looking at the intervention after the second and last incident shows that use of formal social controls increases, but not at the rate that use of informal social controls and leaving do. Over time, the use of police and lawyers remains about the same. This may reflect the responses (or lack of responses) the women got when they did seek help from those sources (Dobash & Dobash, 1977; Fields, 1976; Straus, 1977a).

Seeking outside help varies from a pattern of accepting violence. The responses to this variation influence whether or not this is likely to happen again. Medical doctors, legal professionals, and police officers receive little training in crisis intervention or family violence matters. Thus, when called upon, they often respond inadequately. The case studies that follow provide insight into the effects of inadequate medical and police intervention on the patterns of violence.

In contrast, women increasingly chose to seek help from informal sources, and also to leave the house. Informal social control agents provide support rather than punishment. The informal support provided to women after the most significant and final incidents affected the women's decisions to leave. This support provided a bridging relationship which facilitated both the decision to leave and the ultimate possibilities for change.

The circumstances surrounding the three incidents of violence together indicate that change takes place over time in: (1) the marital status of respondents, (2) the preceding events or stressful situations mentioned, (3) the women's guilt, (4) the women's willingness to "forgive and forget," (5) the evaluation of the violence as part of a pattern versus being an isolated incident, (6) the attributions of responsibility, and (7) the patterns of seeking intervention. Later I will analyze how these changes fit into the overall process of a battered woman's history of violence and her attempts to leave.

THE WOMEN SIX MONTHS LATER

How many women went back to the men after leaving the shelter? What happened to them if they did? What happened if they didn't? To answer these questions, I reinterviewed 24 of the 31 women in the original sample after approximately six months. Of those women, 33% were still married to the men, 25% were separated, and 33% were divorced from the men. Over half of the women (58%) had returned to the man, at least temporarily, after leaving the shelter. Sixteen percent reconciled with the man and then left again. Forty-two percent lived with the man at the time of the follow-up interviews.

Sixty-two percent of the women were employed or full-time students at the time of the second interviews, compared with 35% at the time of the first interviews. Many had gotten help finding jobs from staff at the shelter; some had gotten involved in school programs as a result of referrals made by shelter staff. Of those who had separated or had been divorced, 85% were receiving benefits from A.D.C. and/or from the food stamp program.

Of those who had separated or divorced, the mean income for the six-month period was $2261. Surprisingly, only 50% reported that it had been financially difficult. The fact that the other 50% was equally constrained financially and did not report it as difficult may indicate, as one woman said, "After what I took nothing could be that bad."

All but one of the women had their children, if they had any, with them. In one case the children were in foster care on a temporary basis.

As indicated earlier, violence continued for many of the women. In 54% of the cases, women reported that there had been at least one violent incident. Among those who returned to the partner, 57% reported at least one incident. Of those who returned and later left, 50% reported at least one incident. Those who returned and did not later leave suffered violence in the greatest numbers (62%).

Not returning, however, did not protect the women from violence. Indeed, of the women who never returned to the man, 44% reported at least one violent incident. Physical distance, separate residences, and legal restraining orders did very little to prevent further violence. In one case, the man broke into two different apartments the woman moved to, and one time raped her. The rape resulted in an unwanted pregnancy.

Overall, however, violence decreased. At the first interview, women reported that 100% of the men had been violent in the year prior to their women coming to the shelter. The reduction in percentage of the sample reporting violent incidents does indicate that the intervening stay at the shelter may contribute to reducing levels of violence against women.

The shelter provides both temporary safety and supportive help from experienced staff. The shelter also serves to equalize the power relationship between the men and the women. If the woman has no resources, no place to go, or no money to finance a move, the man has the power advantage. The provision of a place for women to go helps to reduce that power advantage.

Many of the women who returned held the option of a return to the shelter like a trump card, saying to the man, in effect, "If you hit me, I am going to leave, and now I have a place to go." This resource may be enough to change the system—in particular, the pattern of violence.

The case studies that follow provide insight into how this factor and many others contributed to the ongoing process of battering relationships in which the woman tried to leave.

CHAPTER 4

Debbie

Debbie is 26. Her long brown hair is thick and straight. Her voice is quick and lively. She was a client at the shelter for battered women. She stole away while her husband was playing rugby. The arrangements were made very carefully, because he had previously snatched their son when she tried to leave one other time.

Debbie stayed at the shelter with her son, Jesse, for the three-week limit, filed for divorce, got a job as a waitress, and made child care arrangements. Her ability to reorient herself suggested she was self-reliant. She did not struggle as other women often did with fear, indecision, ambivalence, and pain.

When she left the shelter she moved in with another woman and her children, but this did not last. She went back to her husband.

I reinterviewed her six months later under strained conditions in the kitchen of her small house on the outskirts of the city. We started at 10:30 A.M. At 4:00 P.M. she fidgeted and reminded me that her husband would be home from work soon. I left wishing I could freely come back or call her, but I knew I could not. It was too dangerous.

The description that follows is Debbie's life history told in her own words with only minor changes that would protect her identity.

DEBBIE'S LIFE HISTORY

Let's just start with how you met Bob.

Bob had just flown in from Cincinnati. I had gone down to the airport to pick him up. I was going with this boy, and this boy was friends with Bob's brother. They asked me one evening if I wanted to go down to the airport to pick him up, and I said, yes, I'd go. That's how I met Bob. I was still in high school.

After that Bob would come to pick his brother up at school in his Datsun 240Z, which was really neat. I saw that one day and I decided to myself, "Well, I'm going to get a ride in that car." You know how impressionable you are at that age. By and by I did. I met Bob and got a ride in his Z and he liked me right away. I didn't much care for him at the time, but he was very strong-willed and he asked me out, and we started dating.

How old was he?

He was about twenty or twenty-one at that time. He had just come back here to live with his mother. His wife had just—he was married—his wife had just had a baby. He was still married when I met him, but it didn't make . . . it didn't seem to make any difference to me.

Where was his wife?

Cincinnati. She had just had a baby in February and he had left at the end of February that year. I think more or less just to escape from an unhappy marriage, you know, 'cause his wife was pretty dominating, and they fought too.

So school ended and I told Bob, I said, "I'm going out to Colorado," because I had a boyfriend out in Colorado that had been writing to me all year long and I wanted to go out and see him. He said, "Well, I'm going out to Colorado, too, so why don't we go together?" I said, "Oh, okay, fine with me." So we went, and he convinced me to stay with him for a while, and so I did. I did the whole summer.

Was he working at all?

No. We spent the whole summer . . . neither of us worked. We just lived off more or less what he had—what his mother had given him. I didn't know what was going on, but I got pregnant and had a miscarriage in August—end of the summer. After I had the miscarriage, I packed up all my stuff and went down to Santa Fe to see my father.

Without him?

Yes. Without him. 'Cause he had hit me twice, I think.

When was the first time he hit you?

The first time he hit me was in Colorado . . . when we were . . . that summer he had. I don't remember the reason he did . . . he just. . . .

Did he know you were pregnant?

I think he had an idea I was pregnant. He knew more about that stuff than I did, because he already had a wife and a baby. I didn't really know if I was or not. I just didn't really know. I thought maybe I was, and then again I thought, maybe I've just gained weight or something.

Then one morning . . . early one morning I started having pain and I went to the bathroom and I had my miscarriage in the bathroom. And I decided to go down to see my father. I went down to Santa Fe to see my father. He was in pretty bad shape, 'cause he was an alcoholic.

You had lived with your father for a while?

He basically raised us all through our childhood, so he was the main influence in my life as I was growing up. He was the main parent. My mother and father were divorced and then married again and then divorced again. The first time was when I was about five and my father took us to live with my aunt, and then to Santa Fe, and my grandmother took care of us with my father. And then several years later my mom came back and they married again and stayed married for three or four years. I remember something like that, and then the divorce began and I remember feeling very grateful that they had divorced 'cause it just wasn't working out.

And all this time he was drinking? Your father?

He was . . . he had always been a drinker, I guess. In fact, I think that's one reason my mother was fed up with him, and I think he had a temper, too. I don't remember too much about that. I don't remember too much about my mother and father fighting, really. There were a couple of incidents I remember.

Were you beaten as a child?

My father was strict, and we got spankings once in a while, but not often. Just normal, like any other normal child, you know. Not especially bad. From being an alcoholic, you know, and having to accept the responsibility for three kids, you know. He did . . . I think he did a pretty wonderful job.

You had lived with your father for a while?

My last year of high school, my mother and her husband had been stationed here and they asked us if me and my sister wanted to come up here and stay for a while. Me and my sister have always wanted to travel and so we decided, yeah, we will go up there and finish the next year of high school there.

So when you went back, after you had the miscarriage. . . . When you went to your father's, did you tell Bob you were leaving?

No. I didn't. He was asleep, and I had the pain and everything was gone and I just packed my bag and took my suitcases out on the freeway and got a ride.

Why did you leave?

I . . . I don't know why. I just wanted to. It was an opportunity, you know, I had the miscarriage and there was nothing holding me, and I wanted to go down and see my father, and Bob was becoming more and more possessive as the days went by, and I just wanted to leave. I don't know why. I wanted to get away and so. . . .

You said he had hit you by that time?

Yes he did.

Do you remember that?

All I remember was a strong slap to the face and seeing stars, and I don't remember why it happened or anything. It just happened. I was awed. I just couldn't believe it, you know. And I don't remember the circumstances at all. So, me and my father went to see my grandmother, and about a week later I see Bob getting out of the car.

How did he find you there?

He just guessed I guess. I had talked about my grandmother and being raised by her, and he just guessed and came out there and convinced me to come back to Colorado with him. I said, "No, I don't want to."

How did he talk you into it?

He said the things that he . . . I don't remember. He just did. I was very impressionable and. . . .

Did he still have the fancy car?

No. Well, we had a lot of good times together, you know, like we uh . . . he taught me how to rebuild an engine on the car, and we did a lot of fun things together. I just wanted to go see my father and just get away, you know, and then he came after me and I thought, oh boy, this is just like true love. This is really neat. He was coming after me and all this and he told me that he loved me and that he wanted to live together.

He didn't say he wanted to get married?

No. He . . . I had never wanted to get married. Even when we did get married, we didn't want to get married. It was just circumstances. I was pregnant with Jesse. That's how we happened to get married.

What did you do for the couple of years you were talking about before you got married?

We moved around a lot. Stayed in this one place for a while, and then I . . . we met some people and they impressed me and they. . . . It was during that time when drugs were really, you know, popular, and I was, you know, right in the middle of all that, a lot of drugs, not a lot of sex. Bob was the first and stayed the first for a long, long time. And so I just got involved in a lot of drugs and things. Weird things and different things.

I got rid of Bob, and because of that he took all my clothes away from me. Then I was all by myself and didn't have any clothes, nothing, and I called my mother up and asked her if . . . if I could have some money and come back to live with her. I didn't have any clothes. I didn't have nothing. I had to come back here 'cause I didn't have any money or anything.

When I came back up here, you know, I didn't want nothing to do with Bob, but he always pressured me. Finally we got back together again, then we . . . where'd we go? I think out West again. We traveled around a lot.

We did have a lot of fun together, but you know, there were times we did break up, and then get back together, things were okay. He never . . . never did hit me or anything like that. Then when we finally did get married and Jesse was born, I think he became a little jealous of Jesse. I don't know. Shortly after Jesse was born, we started having troubles. That's when they really basically began. Except for that one time back in Colorado.

We decided to get married because of support for me. And boy, wasn't I mad later.

Now I was hooked.

How were you hooked?

Now I was hooked. Things went well for a while and he got this real good job. He got a real good job as a construction worker, and I think that put a lot of pressure on him, because he had to be away for like five days at a time, or three days at a time or whatever, and then come home and be on call still.

So you were kind of alone in the apartment with the baby?

Yes. Quite a bit. And I didn't mind. Whenever Bob and I were together, I've always spent a lot of time by myself. He'd always go out and do what he wanted to do and I always stayed in the apartment. Took care of the house, or worked, or something. And he very seldom worked. It should have told me something back then.

Except for this construction job?

He had this construction job for quite a while, though. He did get laid off for nine months, and then he got called back to work. We really had a lot of plans. He was gonna make a lot of money and he would bring home checks like $500 income a week, and we had a lot of money. I think the job put a lot of pressure on him, and he was jealous of Jesse a little bit.

What happened at the time he was born? Was he with you?

One thing that struck me as really odd was that I got flowers from my mother-in-law and brother-in-law, but I got no flowers from Bob, which I felt was pretty weird. Bob wasn't very attentive to me during that time either. He was always mostly concerned about himself, and what he wanted. Then when Jesse was about eight months I got pregnant again, and I decided to have an abortion because by this time I was figuring out you know, like . . . that Bob was not the husband I really wanted. And then things just started getting worse and worse and worse, and he would come home from his job and start yelling at me and accusing me and. . . .

Accusing you of what?

He always had this big sexual hang-up that I'm not adequate enough and I'm not aggressive enough, and I'm not feminine enough. I do realize that I'm not a very feminine woman because I was raised by my father, you know, and when you're raised by a man you just don't have, you know, he just can't contribute to your femininity at all. I do realize that. I think my father did have a lot to do with that.

But you're very attractive.

I've learned to become more feminine, but my father . . . he had us doing jobs that boys would be doing. We would lift refrigerators and take them out to his truck and move stuff for him, and do all the things boys would do. He had two strong girls so he used us. We've got the strength, and we thought it was great.

It's good training.

It's damn good training. He taught us responsibility, and that you don't have to have a lot of money to get along. We never did have a lot of money and the clothes were never a big thing with us in our life because our father never bought us. . . . Sometimes he would come home with a sweater or something for us, you know, and every time he did it was so . . . it was such a big deal for us, so I think my father contributed a lot to, you know, my not being a very feminine person. Though I did try with Bob. I did try. I read books and tried different things . . . suggestions that books would come up with, you know, and did try to teach myself to be more of an appealing wife in different ways, but it never satisfied him. Always wrong. The yelling came first and then knocking me up against walls and then striking and then, you know, it always got more and more abusive. I finally got fed up with it a few years ago . . . and went for a divorce, but I didn't stay long, that's 'cause I wasn't prepared and didn't have any money.

Can you remember the first time you were hit after Jesse was born?

Can I remember the first time? Yeah. I think it was close to his second birthday. It was after Bob had been called back off his lay-off. I don't remember the reason why he got so upset. I think he grabbed my face and slapped me and pushed me around a little bit, but I don't remember the reason at all. It's really never any real reason for him to behave like that. He just built up anger, and before I knew it he was taking his anger out on me, you know? That's always the way it seemed to work. He just started little by little, you know, and got madder and madder and madder, and before you know it, he was pushing me around and striking me or something.

So, how did you feel?

Very confused. When it really first started happening, I didn't know what was going on. I couldn't figure it out. I stayed with him quite a while when he was doing this, because I like figured out well, maybe he'll come home this time, and I'll do something different. Maybe that might please him and he'll stay off my back. I would always try to do things that . . . that wouldn't make him angry. He was never satisfied. He'd get mad for some stupid reason and take it out on me.

What do you think that is related to?

I think it relates a lot to when he was young and his parents not making him do the things that he should have been doing. I understood that Bob was always the one who got attention from the father. It was always, here's a new gun for you or a new fishing pole for you, and his brother was always in the background. The attention was always drawn toward Bob. Bob was a very exceptional child, as I understand. He could have been . . . he could have been anything. He was intelligent. He was . . . he had a lot of dexterity . . . had a lot of things going for him, but somehow or other, I think through a divorce, and. . . .

That's right. His parents were divorced. How old was he?

I think maybe eight or so. His mother worked a lot, so the boys were left a lot of the time by themselves. Being raised in a big city, I'm sure that had a lot of influence with the way they turned out, too. They lived with their mother but both parents were there. The father would like take them on fishing trips or take them to the zoo, or you know, something. He did . . . I understand he tried.

Was Bob hit as a kid?

Ah, yes. Bob was sort of strong-willed, like about going to school. I remember him telling me they'd have to like beat him to get him out of bed to go to school, or she'd have to go in and turn the mattress upside down, you know, to get him out of bed, you know, or beat him all the way to school to get him to go to school . . . always somehow was . . . always had a lot to do with school. He just didn't want . . . I think he was born with it a lot, you know. Didn't have enough directional guidance . . . enough to stimulate to thinking, 'cause he was very intelligent, as I understand, as a child.

It was funny. Me and him took an IQ test a couple of weeks ago and we came out with the same IQ. 135. I was surprised. I understand when I was a child I had an IQ test and it was 135. As I understand, it's not bad. So it makes me so mad, you know, 'cause neither one of us have put this intelligence thing to any really creative thing, you know. I don't have any specific training and neither does Bob, but we're both very capable of doing just about anything we want to do and here we are in low-middle-class income . . . still not having any direction in our life because it's always been a battle more or less between me and Bob.

You know, there are times when things go so good, and then they get bad and I leave, you know, and then I'll come back to him and it'll go fine again, and then it will get bad again and I'll leave. Been this way for eight years.

So the first time he hit you after you got married was after Jesse was born?

It was then that I decided to go for a divorce.

So what did you actually do?

Well, I got ahold of one of my friends and asked her if I could come and stay with her. Jesse was about one or two. I took Jesse with me and I didn't have any money . . . didn't have any car . . . didn't have anything, really. I stayed I think a week, and then decided to go back to Bob, 'cause he convinced me to go back with him too, and I decided to do that because I just really wasn't prepared for the whole ordeal. So I went back and planned it all out. I got ahold of a car and saved my money, bought extra groceries, and prepared myself for it. So about Mother's Day, Bob left to go out on the road and I went back to the house and packed up all my stuff, got my money, and got all the extra food, and got in contact with the girl that was gonna sell me the car and everything . . . went back over to the same girl's house and really made an effort to get a divorce and . . . tried to get what I wanted. You know?

Yes.

And that backfired on me because when Bob came back several weeks later, he had an operation on his eye. He asked me if he could have Jesse for a couple of weeks. I thought, "This is really nice of him," 'cause, you know, it gave me a chance to get myself all situated with a job and baby-sitting for Jesse and everything. I thought, "This

is really nice of him." The day of the divorce he didn't show up in court
and that was the day he was supposed to bring Jesse back to me, and he
wasn't in court and the lawyer said, "Where's he at?" I said, "I don't
know." I went back to the apartment and everything was gone including Jesse.

You didn't have any suspicion he was going to do this?

No. I remember him saying he was going to leave, gonna go
someplace. He didn't say where, but he was gonna leave. He didn't
say, "I'm taking Jesse with me." He did not say that. He tells me he did
say that, but he didn't, 'cause if he did say that to me, I would have
become very panicky and tried to get Jesse at that time and the whole
bit. I wouldn't have just sat there. He didn't. He said he did tell, but he
didn't tell me. He told me in a roundabout way, you know, beating
around the bush, he did tell. . . .

He didn't let you know where he was with Jesse?

No. I waited a whole month, and I called up, and his mother
would say, "I do not know where they are. I have not seen them. I do
not know where they're at." What was I supposed to say? Okay. Fine. I
called up again the next week. "They're not here. I haven't seen or
heard from him." I got suspicious, you know, I thought, "They've got
to be up there." I quit my job and came up here and they were there. He
made a promise to me, you know, again, that he would bring Jesse
back to me in August . . . uh, no, in September . . . so I went back,
got another job, saved money, got a nice duplex with a yard for us, nice
floors and the whole thing . . . bought furniture, stove and refriger-
ator, table and chairs, waited until November. Finally got fed up with
waiting, packed up all my stuff, quit my job, took my money out of the
bank and came up here. And boy wasn't that hell. Finally ended up at
the beach and got a job down there. It became too much of a hassle the
way he treated me when I tried to come over to see Jesse, and usually
Jesse wasn't there. I ended up having a fight with his mother one
evening.

Tell me about that.

I just got fed up with the whole thing 'cause nobody would let me
see him. Nobody would . . . they were always telling me lies, you
know, and nobody would compromise with me, and I just got fed up so
I thought I would use the same things. I'd steal Jesse like he stole Jesse
from me. So I went over . . . I found out Bob was playing tennis that
night and obviously Jesse was over at my mother-in-law's, so I went
over there and got inside, and tried to talk very rationally to her. I tried
to tell her, "You've got to understand, Bob has not been treating me

good." I didn't go into a lot of detail 'cause I was trying to get Jesse away from her at the same time, and she got very pissed off at me, and she started yelling at me, "Don't ever call me anything. Don't call me Hester. Don't call me Mom. Don't call me anything. My name is Mrs. Moore." To this day I don't call her anything but Mrs. Moore because of that night. And so she started . . . she got up and started . . . she's very tall and she was just all over. She struck me a couple of times, and I tried to get out the door with Jesse. It was a struggle on account of the door and finally she just . . . I didn't want to hit her. I didn't want to do anything to her even though she was abusing me. I just didn't want to do that. It's not my nature to be that, but she was just all over, and I had gotten fed up and I pushed her away from me and she went up against the door and broke the storm door and glass went flying everywhere.

It was my opportunity, and I grabbed Jesse and ran out the door and she came out after me, and we got into a big bear hug. She just enclosed me with her arms and it was like . . . like a tug of war with Jesse, and Jesse was just screaming and carrying on and I tried to get my knee up her [mother-in-law's] crotch a couple of times, but she was just so much taller than me I couldn't reach. Finally Jesse was just getting so upset and I let go. She ran back into the house with Jesse, and I sat in the car and smoked for a few minutes and cried a little bit and went back up to the door. She wouldn't answer the door. She had the doors locked. And I thought I had better get out of there before she called the police.

Did you ever try to do anything legally?

I began to get ahold of a lawyer. I tried twice to take Jesse and it didn't work, so I finally decided to use a lawyer which I should have done the minute I got up there, but I didn't. We proceeded with the divorce papers and all that. Then Bob got ahold of me one night, and he told me he was leaving again with Jesse. I panicked. I came back to him a couple of days later. I said, "Okay, Bob, we'll make an agreement and I'll stay here." So we did and that's . . . after that, that was the worst. That was the worst it had ever gotten, after I came back to live with Bob.

What do you mean it got worse?

The abuse got worse.

Tell me about that.

The first time after I came back was immediately after I got a job and Bob was . . . Bob's mom was supporting him basically, 'cause he was not working, or he had been working off and on. I got a job and I got food stamps so his mom wouldn't have to support us. I was very vindictive toward her 'cause she had lied to me. She had hit me and everything, and she accused me of being a tramp and all kinds of things. So I didn't want to have nothing to do with her. Didn't want her supporting us. Didn't want her feeding us or anything. 'Course I'm that way anyway. You know, my father taught us to be very independent.

I worked for seven months, and all through this time he didn't trust me, and he thought I had been running around with other men.

It took him two weeks after I came back before he hit me, and it was really bad. I was sitting over there and for no reason he came up and just knocked me over in the chair. I went down. Me and the chair went down, and he started knocking me all over the kitchen, and down the hall here, and pushed me and I scraped my arm, and he pushed me into that thing right there, and I scraped my arm real bad. I asked him if I could wash my arm off 'cause it was bleeding a little bit and he said, "No." Then I went into the bedroom, and he started knocking me around the bedroom. I was up against the door, and he slapped my face, and I hit my head on the door sill, and a big bump came up. I said, "Can I go wash my face?" and he said, "No." It scared me because a big bump just immediately rose, and that scared me. Then he knocked me down and kicked me a couple of times, and finally he just walked out. I had bruises all over me, on my face and on my arms, on my legs, and . . . I couldn't go right to work.

I remember one day I had a split shift, and they wanted me to stay and fix up the banquet room, and I said okay, and I called up Bob and I said, "You don't have to pick me up 'cause they want me to stay and fix up the banquet room," and then after I called him, two other girls had come in that were working the banquet to set it up, so then I called him back to say "Well, you got to pick me up," but I couldn't get ahold of him, 'cause he was out playing tennis or something. So I thought he wasn't going to come and pick me up, and this girl that I was working with asked me if I wanted to go to her house and have a drink and just wait for two hours and then come back for the second shift. I said, "Why not?"

Well, he had come to pick me up and he waited the two hours for me to come back from this girl's house, 'cause he thought I was out doing something else. When I came back for my second shift, he was just so angry. Just so angry at me. He was yelling at me, "Get into the Jeep," and I didn't want to get into the Jeep, 'cause I knew what would happen. It was a big scene. Great big scene. So we came back here. I didn't want to get out of the Jeep, I was hanging on the bar that we have

inside. The neighbors ended up calling the cops. He was trying to get
me out of the Jeep, my neighbors saw this. He was pulling my hair and
hitting me and trying to get me out of the Jeep, and I just didn't want
to get out. I knew the minute we got inside, it would be worse.

What exactly did the police do?

When the cops drove into the yard, Bob went back and talked to
them. When he came back, he said, "Oh, one of them was my friend."
Therefore, they did not come up and ask me how I was. They did not ask
me if I wanted any help. They just talked to Bob and left.

All my neighbors were very upset. They were so mad. They wanted
to see Bob get into trouble, 'cause they had seen several things. Sometimes I would run out of the house and go stand over there on that
porch, because it was wide open. I thought sure he can't do nothing out
in the open. I would stand there, and he would yell at me and things
like that, but I thought it was safe over there.

I've always been a faithful wife and I've always kept the house
clean. I've always tried to do special things for Bob, you know. I've
always considered myself a good wife. Maybe not perfect, but, you
know, an adequate enough wife. Especially after putting up with all
his nonsense.

*There was one time you told me about that seemed really critical to
you.*

Oh yeah, that was so strange. I don't remember what brought it
on. It was something to do with work. See Bob was not working and he
would not take care of Jesse. He wanted me to work, because he didn't
trust me enough to stay here and take care of Jesse by myself while he
worked. So I had to work while he stayed home and did nothing. I
worked plus took care of Jesse in the evenings and the housework and
all. I mean everything. I had to live like that, because it was either that
or him take Jesse away from me. I had to go along with it. I had to,
'cause I didn't want him taking Jesse away from me.

That one time it was really strange. I think we had been fighting
before that, too. So we went and picked up Jesse and then flew past the
house. I said, "Where're you going?" He said, "Well, I'm going to take
you out to . . . I'm gonna take you somewhere and I'm gonna teach
you a lesson." I said, "But Bob, Jesse's in the back seat." He turned
around and he said to Jesse, "Well, you know, Jesse, your mother is
nothing but a lying bitch—a lying cold bitch." I couldn't believe this.
He was telling Jesse this, you know, about me and 'course I couldn't do
nothing about it. Jesse was starting to get upset. Bob drove us to the
next town out on this kind of, like, deserted road. He stopped and I got

out of the Jeep, and he got out of the Jeep, and he raised his fist to me a couple of times and each time I'd duck. One thing I would do a lot is if he raised his fist, I would just roll up into a ball, you know, to protect my head or whatever. I crouched down on the ground and covered myself up. Jesse was getting hysterical, I was barefooted, too, and he was gonna leave me there to walk and to think things over—like I really had been doing something bad and he was punishing me. He left me there a couple of times, but he came back each time. Each time he'd start yelling at me and calling me names, and telling Jesse what a bad mother I was and everything. Finally he said, "Well, you just get in the Jeep and we'll go home and settle this." Then he turned around and he got a flat tire, so we had to hitchhike back to town. Then when we got to town his mother was at McDonald's and he said, "Okay, let's just call this quits. It's fine. It's over with." So I said, "Okay, it's over and finished with." You know, I thought it was over and finished with. He had to go to his mother's to get his spare tire 'cause it was in her garage. After all that was taken care of, he started in on me again. "We're gonna finish this up." I don't remember the rest of the evening. I'm sure it was just yelling and screaming and maybe a few, you know, pushing around. . . .

But that really made an impression on you?

Oh well, it sure did. I mean, you know, telling my son what a lousy mother I am and I'm nothing but a lying cold bitch really bothered me. He always exaggerated things, you know. I did lie to him a couple of times, just more or less for self-preservation. There was no great big lies that made a great big difference in our whole life.

Like what?

Like writing letters to my mother. He'd ask me, "Are you telling your mother about stuff like this?" and I'd say, "No, I don't write her about things like that," but I did. I wrote to her and said I'm not too happy and I'm having a little bit of problems, and she'd write back to me. I'd told her, "Don't say nothing about this in your letter," you know, but a couple of times she did and Bob would read it and he'd get very upset. I just wanted her to give me a couple of words of encouragement or an unbiased opinion or something.

He didn't want anybody to know he was doing this?

No. He didn't want me having nothing to do with my mother.

How about other people?

Oh, I was not allowed to have friends. Not allowed to go anywhere with Jesse by myself. This was why it was so bad, 'cause he told me he didn't trust me, therefore I couldn't go places with Jesse by myself, or I couldn't go to the store with Jesse, or I couldn't spend time with Jesse, or I couldn't go out and have any kind of relationship with any girls, or I couldn't do anything. Not unless he gave me permission, and so forth and so on.

I remember when you told me about how you had to plan to come to the shelter.

Ya, he just never trusted me. Well, after a while, you know, after seven months of living with me, he finally let me go out with the girls drinking after work. We went to the beach, which is really about half-an-hour, forty-five minutes' drive from here, and I didn't get back until three o'clock in the morning, which is all perfectly innocent. Nothing happened.

I came back at three o'clock in the morning. All my clothes were out on the porch, and the door was locked. I had to go spend the night with somebody else. Then I went to work that next day and he came to get me at work and brought me back here. I said, "I'm not working any more. You go to work. I'm fed up. You just keep embarrassing me at my job." So I quit my job, 'cause I just had had it. He had embarrassed me too many times. Five or six times I had walked into work with bruises on me, and they'd ask, "How did you do that?" I said, "I fell down the steps," you know, or something. One girl knew about it, though. I had to confide in somebody, you know. I felt the need to. Things basically began to settle down a little bit and Bob got a job I think a month later. Not very quick. They got a little bit smoother, 'cause I had started to prove to him that I could be trusted, he began to put a little bit of faith in me, so he went to work. . . .

There were a few other incidents, you know, and I had. . . . In November, I went to see Cynthia, my social worker, 'cause I was just, you know, being very depressed. I'd sit here at the table and cry for no reason and I was always very depressed, 'cause things still weren't normal. So I went to see Cynthia and I saw her two times and she advised me to get out for my own benefit, which was so surprising to me. I just couldn't believe it, you know. I think she had mentioned it, or somebody had mentioned that there was a new program out, and it was for a place to go for women. I don't remember how I got all the information, but somehow I had. My friend was helping me, and I'd go up to her house and make phone calls. I was really doing it through her so there would be nothing coming through here, you know, that he would become suspicious of. They asked me a few questions, and I answered them, and they said, "Yes, you're eligible to come to the shelter," and I said, "Okay," I said, "I don't know when I can or

anything like that. I'll just have to let you know." So during the time
when I was waiting, I packed up a few things. I hid them over there,
and once again, tried to take care of some loose ends, so that when I got
ready to go, I could just pick it all up and go.

One Sunday Bob went to play rugby, and I decided that was it.
That was the night I called them and they said, "Yes, we have room for
you," and I called a taxi to come pick me up here. God, it took an
eternity. The taxi took half-an-hour to get here and Diane was waiting
for me. The taxi took me there, and we unloaded all my stuff into her
car and she took me to the shelter. As I understand, I just missed Bob by
the skin of my teeth, because he had felt something was happening, so
he just left the rugby game in the middle of the whole thing—and went
over to his mom's and got his mom and came back over here. I guess I
had just missed him. He went into the bathroom and saw the tooth-
brushes gone, and he knew something was . . . we had left again.

*During the time you were at the shelter, you didn't tell him where
you were?*

Not until the last week or so, 'cause I didn't . . . I just knew the
minute I got in contact with him, a lot of confusion would come about
and a lot of, you know, weird things would happen. I just didn't want
him to know. I didn't contact him for a while, and as I understand it,
everyone was going into nervous fits. So I was peaceful a little while,
you know. His mother was having a nervous breakdown, which I
didn't care. He was having a nervous breakdown, which I didn't care. I
just really didn't care. In fact, I thought, well, he deserved it in a way,
for all the things he did to me.

So you contacted your husband. What did you say to him?

While I was at the shelter I had divorce papers drawn up. After he
got the divorce papers, I had called him, because then he knew I was in
the city. I figured I might as well call him, you know, so I knew he was
all right and everything. We arranged a couple of meetings with each
other. Cynthia wanted us to do that to build up some trust between us,
you know.

*So you did see him. You did see Bob. Did you see him with
Cynthia?*

One time. What a great disaster that was. It was on a Monday, I
think. I was very tired, really tired, 'cause I had been doing a lot, you
know, trying to get everything organized. Working and everything at
the same time. We went to see her at her office, and I was so tired I
just. . . . Anything Bob would say I just cried, you know, and we

couldn't come to an agreement of, like letting Jesse come here for three days, but I let him come.

On Wednesday, I came here to visit him, and I had to be back at work at eight o'clock. It was getting time to go. I said, "Well, I've got to go. I've got to get back and get ready for work." He wasn't going to let me go. It started getting closer and closer to eight o'clock and finally I picked up and started to walk out, and he wouldn't let me out of the house. Physically he wouldn't let me out of the house. It became more or less a wrestling match. Finally I knew I couldn't get out of there so I called up work and said, "I can't make it in there tonight." I was very upset.

Thursday, the next day, was my birthday, and I went into work and the boss told me, "If you ever do that again, you're going to lose your job. You know you've got to make arrangements." I said, "I know that. I'm sorry, but you have to understand." I tried to explain it to him —as little as I could—tried to give him what was basically happening.

That night Bob showed up. It was my birthday. He wanted to take me out for breakfast. I agreed just to pacify him. He was there at closing, and he went out to the Jeep to wait for me. He was getting mad. He was slowly getting mad. I couldn't figure out why. There was really no reason for him to be getting agitated, but he was. So we went around the corner and parked the Jeep, got out, and these two drunks came walking by us. One of the drunks said something to Bob. Bob was getting so agitated, he said something, and before I knew it, the three of them were in a big fight. I was just so dumbfounded and so paranoid, you know, at two o'clock in the morning on the waterfront, three guys are fighting. I turned around and went back to work and knocked on doors to let me in and I tried to explain to my boss. I said, "We've got to call the police." He started giving me a lecture, "You obviously care very much about this man," and I was getting mad. I listened to him for a while, then I just walked out—went back to the restaurant and nobody was there.

So I went and called a taxi and went back to my apartment and looked first for the Jeep. It wasn't there, and I thought, "Well, I'm safe, I'll go in and go to sleep, and maybe it will be better tomorrow."

So I go into . . . we had like a hall . . . and there he was sitting on the bench, and I knew he was just so mad at me. He was furious, because he had gotten into a fight with those two drunks, and they had done a lot of damage to the Jeep. Of course, he blamed it all on me. He was just at the peak of his anger. He started spitting at me and threw a pack of cigarettes at me, telling me, "You've got to make up your mind right now. If you don't come with me right now, you're going to regret it." Just like before, threatening me with Jesse. If I don't do what he wants me to do he will make me pay by taking Jesse away from me. I stood my ground for as long as I could, you know. I didn't want to go back. I tried to be as willful as I could. But, I gave in. I couldn't take it. He kept telling me, "You've got to make up your mind right now, because if you don't make up your mind right now, if you don't come back with me right now, you're going to be very sorry." 'Course I always take those threats from what he says because he did do it. He has done it. So, I did. I gave in. I felt so bad because it was not what I wanted. I tried to explain to Bob that it would be better if he just waited until . . . if we could just see each other and then when things got better maybe we'd go back to living with each other, but he had to give me time, you know, to get over me being afraid of him, and he had to build up some trust in me. He wouldn't accept it. He didn't want it that way. He wanted me there . . . here. So I gave in to him.

Why do you think he wants you here?

I am his security. I am what keeps him together. He's basically very insecure. He wants very much to have a family and have a wife . . . and have the normal things that people do. He wants it very badly and he loves me a lot.

So you've been back here a little over five months.

And when I came back here, we had an agreement. It would be around six months on a trial basis. I knew it was like talking out the window, 'cause I knew it wouldn't really, you know, he wouldn't stick to an agreement that he's made. The agreement was that if he didn't prove to me that he could control his temper and not threaten me and keep a job and keep his responsibilities, that he would pack up his bags and leave. That was the agreement.

Of course I had to go along with it, because he had put me in the position. I really felt he put me in a bind over at my apartment. So he agreed to it, and I agreed to it . . . and here it is almost six months later, and he has kept basically his agreement. So I guess here I am.

He has not directed his anger at me but one time.

What happened that one time?

He started slapping Jesse around, and he was wet 'cause he had been swimming. Bob was pretty drunk. His mother lit into him just really heavy because he was slapping Jesse around while he was wet. This was one of the times she got to see how erratic he becomes over nothing. He got madder and madder and madder. Pretty soon it was a big fight—all three of us. Then I was sitting in the chair. I told him, "I'm not going home until you settle down, you know," so he come over to me and he raised—drew back his fist and I started to become very hysterical.

What do you mean—hysterical?

I just started crying a lot and sobbing and the whole thing. She got in between us. The he again came at me, walked over to the chair and he kicked the chair. I was in a recliner . . . and he kicked the chair, but at the same moment I thought he was going to kick me and I raised my leg and kicked him, very, you know, adolescent stuff. After I kicked him, he was furious, so he hit me on the leg. So I became very hysterical. He touched me once again and I went all out of control. She had to give me a Valium to settle down.

Whenever he doesn't get his way he becomes very irrational, and also the alcohol aggravates the whole situation too.

Is he violent only when he's drinking?

No. It seems to be more often when he's drinking. Drinking seems to touch it off more—more intensity. But that time he took me out of town and left me he hadn't had a drink, and that time he knocked me all around the house, he had not been drinking.

Is he drinking more regularly now than he was before?

No. It's not too bad. After work he buys himself a six-pack, drinks it throughout the night, maybe goes out to buy another one, and maybe drinks two or three out of that. One week, I think it was after that episode at her house, he told me that he could stop drinking. He stopped drinking for a whole week, and I was really impressed that he was able to do that. But, you know, he started drinking a little bit more. Then he was telling me the other day, he thinks he has figured it out— his point where too much drinking will make him violent. He said something like, "Eight beers on an empty stomach is about all I think I can handle, and if I eat and drink, I can drink all day long." He's been trying to rationalize it out a little bit in his own mind, that point between rationality and irrationality. He's trying, but I think he still needs help.

How does he feel about getting help?

I said to him one day something about getting help, and he said, "I ain't never going to do that again. I ain't going to see nobody." I think he feels embarrassed, or ashamed or something.

So, what do you think is going to happen?

You'll see, it will probably be the same thing over again. It'll go smooth for a while and things will work out for a while and then progressively they'll start, maybe he'll start, you know, he's started already by losing his temper—not with me—but he still lost his temper very badly. So it's like a ladder to me. It starts with this, then it goes to the next step, then to the next, then pretty soon, it's right back where it was. I've been through this three times to try to get him divorced—get him away from me, try to settle the thing out. I come right back, and it will start out okay for a couple of weeks, then it will start right back again. Okay, this time it's taken him a little bit longer, 'cause I think he had a little bit more understanding of what has happened to himself. But I think eventually it will just be like it was before, though he knows, because I told him before and I really seriously mean it, if he does really hurt me, I will file assault charges. It may take me twenty-four hours to get to it, but I will. That day he hit me on the leg at his house, or his mother's house, I didn't really consider that because I hit him first. I mean I struck out at him first. It was just like an automatic thing for him, so I don't really consider that an abuse, more or less, you know, it's just that a lot of things were happening. But if he ever did come at me, and I told him . . . he knows that I will. He almost expects it . . . to come.

What do you think you want?

What do I want? I want a life of my own. I want to be independent. I want to find something to do with my life and I don't want nobody telling me what to do. I'm pretty self-sufficient if I want to be. It's just that my weakness is facing Bob. He knows how to get to me. He knows how to manipulate me.

How?

By Jesse and by his forcefulness in placing all this fear on me. He knows how to use me. I can't ever see having what I want until Jesse gets to be maybe thirteen or so. I'm not saying I could take it until Jesse is thirteen. I could take Bob. I mean, I could live with him just as long as he doesn't lash out at me. I can play the game. I can play the role. I can do it. Just as long as he doesn't attack me or. . . .

The shelter is impressed upon Bob's mind. It really made a big impression on Bob's mind that there are people out there that want to help people—help women in this situation, and there is a place that I can go, that if it ever got too bad, that I don't have to stay here. And that's a threat to him, or that holds him in his place in a way.

What do you think the shelter gave you?

The shelter gave me a little peace of mind for a while, which I really needed at the time, because like I said, I was very depressed. It gave me time to sort of get myself out of that. I think if I could have got what I wanted, I would have been very very very grateful. I am still very grateful, even though I did mess it up.

Was there anything that could have given you support so that you wouldn't have gone back at that time?

No. If I could have stayed at the shelter a year. If I could have stayed there long enough to go through the divorce. . . . You know what I mean? So that I would have that protection, 'cause once I got out of there I didn't have that protection that I think a lot of women need to get over that divorce period.

Getting an apartment took away that protection I had, where Bob couldn't come after me, and he couldn't come into my house and scream at me, and try to talk me out of it and all this kind of stuff. I really wish that I could have stayed there until the divorce was final, because I was very vulnerable at that point, you know. I was very vulnerable toward Bob. If I could have stayed there until the divorce was final that would really have impressed upon Bob what I was really after. But he knew he could get me if he could just get me away from . . . if he could just get me away from . . . like that Wednesday night. But that's an awful lot to ask, you know, from somebody who protects. . . . That's an awful long time to say, "Protect me for three months until my divorce is over." And then again you sound like a child or like you're not capable of handling your own situation, really. But sometimes it is hard to handle a situation like that. I really did want what I had after I left the shelter. I thought I had it. I was starting really well. We found a fairly decent place to live and the bus gave me the opportunity to get a good job, and everything. But, I felt that I was put in the position that just didn't really give me any choice.

CHAPTER 5

Elizabeth

Elizabeth is 30. She is a gay, fun-loving folk dancer. Many nights during her first stay she entertained other women at the shelter. Elizabeth also thinks about committing suicide. At these times, her dancing becomes that of a little girl, and this woman who is approximately 5′9″ curls herself over her body.

Elizabeth is in the process of sorting out a series of sexually and physically victimizing relationships that date back to her childhood. Her repeated relationships with men who were abusive would lead some to label Elizabeth masochistic. She did not enjoy the abuse, however, and she did not seek it out. Elizabeth learned early in life not to respond when she was hurt, and that learned pattern continued in later abusive relationships.

Elizabeth has three children. The oldest, born when Elizabeth was a teenager, is being raised by her mother. Elizabeth put the others in temporary foster care because she was worried about her ability to cope during those periods when she is overcome with feelings of worthlessness, fear, and anger.

What follows is Elizabeth's life history in her own words starting with her description of her father. Editing changes have been made to protect her identity.

ELIZABETH'S LIFE HISTORY

What work did your father do, Elizabeth?
He unloaded cargo off the boats and then loaded stuff back on, fish or whatever. He mostly worked with the fishermen. He used to drink a lot.
Do you remember that?
We would watch for him, coming down over the hill. Whoever could get to the phone first, you know, would get a nickel to call the cops on our father. We'd race to the phone, see who could call first. We

would get the nickel to call the cops on our own father. That's the way it was, because my mother would be ascared when he came home drinking.

When the cops came to help, what did they do?

Automatically they would take him, you know, and arrest him unless he was passed out or something and not doing anything then. They couldn't do anything about it once he was in the house when he was passed out or something like that.

One time my father came down over the hill, and he was laughing 'cause he had called the cops on himself. They knew him so well from him going there all the time, you know, from being drunk. He just called them up and said, "This is Tommy. I'm drunk again. Come and get me." He came down over the hill laughing and said, "Well, you don't get the nickel today. I called them on the phone." He was dancing down over the hill, you know.

Your mother called the cops because she was afraid that he would hit her?

Ah, well, she, but my mother . . . my father never really hit my mother that I ever knew unless it happened way back before I was born. I haven't any knowledge that my father had ever hit her. Maybe just once. It was more foul language, you know.

Did he ever hit the kids?

I don't remember . . . I don't remember offhand him hitting the kids, no. My father used a razor belt as far as discipline goes. He always used to do things like talk to us, more or less sit down and rave at you for about an hour or so, and you had to sit there and listen, you know. You didn't get up and go until you could go. He'd say, "You listen to me." Maybe in an hour or two you could go off.

How about your mother?

My mother never interfered. Me and my mother are . . . don't have much of a relationship. I can't explain it. I never felt like you could talk to my mother. I don't know whether it was having so many children or what it was, but I never remember her hugging us, or telling me she loved me. No, I didn't feel it.

But you did feel it from your father?

I felt my father loved me and cared about me. You could feel in a sense that he cared. Once in a while he would hug you or fool with you or take you someplace which would show love. My mother more or less kept alone, off to herself. I can remember her crying a lot.

I always felt worried about not feeling loved by my mother, and how much I wanted to be. Just before I came here, I talked to my mother on the phone. I felt I could talk to her on the phone, but in person I can't talk to her at all. Over the phone I was talking to her, and I said, "I don't know how to say this, but, I love you, and I felt strange at times when I wanted to go to you and hug you and everything, but I thought you would send me off to school or out to play or something." I told my mother this, "Maybe you feel the same way. I don't know." I said, "Maybe you feel like you want to do this too, but you're afraid to."

And what did she say?

She said, "Yeah, sometimes I felt that way." I said, "Well, I can remember that you said that your mother never told you that she loved you, that you never felt love from her. You didn't say that much about it toward me or some of the others. Maybe it's because you just didn't know how." I was trying to tell her there was a terrible feeling I had, and she came right over and she hugged me and she told me she loved me. That was a good feeling, having her arms around me. That was really nice.

I've always felt like she was cold. I've always felt like she didn't really care about me, because I never felt her. I could never talk to her or I never . . . she never took me aside to talk to her. I never heard her say, "I love you."

I think she was unhappy for a lot of years. I think because her first child died. He was stillborn.

Having someone to talk to about it might have stopped her from dreaming about it. But he [the father] was gone all the time. He went to the hospital for a while. Mostly he would just come home for supper, and then he'd leave again. I remember her saying, "I wish you'd stay home more often."

Was she unhappy then?

She didn't feel a need to reach out. I didn't feel her reaching out to us 'til we wanted to reach out to her. I think I wanted that. I didn't know how the rest felt. I know I wanted to touch her but I was scared to touch her. Afraid she might reject me. I was waiting for her, you know, to show some sign that it was all right.

You talked about your father, how he would go out and play and be lively?

Yeah. My father, he was lively. He would sing and dance and used to always play the harmonica. He was playful singing to us. He showed love in some ways.

I don't remember my mother doing that. I don't. I think she wanted to. She was left with the house and all the responsibility. Now I think she regrets the fact that she didn't do more.

Did you have girl friends when you were in school?

No. I was more or less on my own—that kind of girl. There was a couple of girls that I used to chum with, not for too long, though. For a while I tried to be friends with them, but, I don't know, I more or less stuck around just with my family. That's what this family does. I think most of us never really knew how to play.

Is that when you began to get interested in dancing?

No. I used to swing all the time. I used to go out, go down to the playground, swing on the swings, way up high and sing as loud as I could sing. I was into singing more than I was anything else. I would swing, singing way up high in the air. Yeah. Swing way up high and sing that song, "When the world hits your eye like a big pizza pie, that's amora." You know, stuff like that. It was funny. Other kids would come down and try to sing. They would try to sing with me. I'd race down and try to get the first swing where I wanted to swing. My usual swing you know, and I'd swing up high and they'd start swinging up high with me, and before you know it, I had everybody on the whole swing screaming.

One day I had to leave the playground and leave everybody. I went home with awful pains in my side. You know, like an appendix attack. I got down and started walking off. I could barely walk. I was doubled over all the way home.

How old were you?

Twelve I think. Twelve or thirteen. I got home, and I went in on the bed, and I was crying out loud. My mother said, "If you don't stop your crying, I'm gonna take you to the doctor." Now I didn't want to go to the doctor's. I did not want to go. You know, the stories I heard about doctors scared me to death about the doctor. I didn't want to go no matter how much it hurt, but I kept hollering and hollering, 'cause it hurt more and more and more, and getting worse. Finally at the end of the day my mother said, "I'm gonna take you to the doctor's." So I got up and I got dressed, and when I got up there, all I remember is the doctor saying, "You're very lucky you brought her in now. Her appendix is just about ready to burst." I guess when I went to the hospital it did burst. My mother said she almost lost me in that hospital.

My mother was a funny woman. She'd take me to the doctor's when something was wrong, or something like that, but she would seem like she thought that you didn't know what you were saying. She'd wave at you to go away, you know, but if anything was wrong, she'd get you to the doctor. Most of the time you'd cover up and say nothing's wrong with you.

How did you feel about that?

Kind of that they don't believe you. It didn't help when I was younger, either. My older brother used to come home drinking, I guess, and came upstairs into my room. I was sleeping, and he ripped the covers off me and had his hands on me where they should not be. He was undressed and when I came to and saw him, I was just shocked. You know, I wanted to scream out, but I didn't dare to. Finally he went out of the room and said, "Please don't tell Mama. Please don't tell Mama. I didn't mean to do it. Please don't tell." And all the time I wanted to go downstairs and tell my mother and father, but I was scared to death of my own brother who was trying to harm me and not say anything. He might try to kill me or hurt me. I couldn't say anything, and so I'm lying there wide awake waiting for him to go to sleep, hoping, you know, that people are sleeping when I do make my move to get downstairs and see my mother and father. So eventually I did get out and went downstairs and told them.

You did tell your parents?

I went in and told my mother and father. They said, "Oh, no. That's awful," or something.

And what did they do?

They said, "We'll talk to Jimmy in the morning." They said, "Don't say anything to him. We'll talk to him. Now go back to bed and try to get some sleep." I didn't dare to go back upstairs, so I slept down on the couch.

And did they talk to him?

I don't know for sure if they did talk to him, because I wasn't there, and they never told me if they did talk to him, and I didn't bother to ask him or nothing afterwards. But I used to see my brother, right, every morning like I say. We used to do these things together, but from then on I carried an awful feeling toward my brother when I saw him. Every time for years, I'd try to talk to him, and I couldn't.

Do you see him now?

One night we were all at a club, and I finally blurted it out. Got feeling good, you know, and I told him I hated him. I said, "I hate you for what you've done to me," and I went home—got a ride home with my sister, but on the way home I felt bad for what I said. The thing I couldn't understand, either, is that my brother degraded me badly. He degraded me for quite a few years after that thing happened. Even today that bothers me.

My mother didn't know about the thing with those guys either.

Tell me about that.

These boys picked me up and were going to give me a ride home. They took me for a ride and made me do all kinds of things. They didn't take my virginity. They didn't touch me in that way, but they made me do all kinds of weird things to them while the others watched. They shut the car door and made me do all kinds of things. This was before I was even married.

My mother used to send me over to my sister's every night and this was when that thing happened, when I was coming home, at nighttime.

They dropped me off afterwards, but I was so petrified, I didn't feel I could tell anybody. I was so scared and so ashamed about what happened. I figured they wouldn't tell nobody, and I didn't tell nobody either.

You never told anybody?

I held it inside for a long time. I didn't dare tell nobody, especially my mother and father. I was afraid they would blame me.

You could have told somebody who at least one of these guys was?

I know that I knew one of them guys, but I cannot place him in my mind. I know at that time I knew one of those guys. I just can't . . . but I know that one of them I knew. Maybe it was someone I really cared about, and I probably don't want to remember anyway. I don't know, but I know that I recognized one of those people. The other ones I didn't know. I can't even remember their faces.

Do you think about that a lot?

This is what bothers me about the different guys that I see hanging around on the corners. This is probably why I'm scared in public. Afraid in public. This could be why I feel so uneasy in public. I think I really would rather have known who they were than not know, because at least I would know when I see them, I wouldn't feel. . . . Sometimes I wish I could remember. I think about that a lot of times. It took me fifteen years to tell anybody about that. I did tell the man I am married to now, but I didn't tell either of my other husbands.

How old were you, Elizabeth, when you got married the first time?

Seventeen.

How did you meet him?

I'm confused. At a New Year's Eve celebration. I kind of liked him, but I don't know if it was love or not. Even today I don't know what love is. Back then I think it was more like infatuation.

How did you decide to get married?

Well, I ended up getting pregnant and I thought that if I didn't marry him, I wouldn't be able to keep my child. My mother never talked to me. I thought I would lose Donny if I didn't have the baby. This was why I had him.

How did your mother react when she knew you were pregnant?

She thought it was absolutely right that I did marry him, because I was gonna have his child.

Was she angry at you?

I couldn't tell her. I stayed away from the house for a whole week. I went to my older sister. I told her. My older sister went and told my mother. I didn't dare go home. My father raved at me, "How could you do this to your mother?" I went into the other room and my mother was crying, and I guess she had been upset since I had been gone. One thing led to another and she said, "How come you had to go and tell Amy of all people instead of telling me yourself?" It seemed there was a conflict between my mother's [younger] children and my sister Amy's children. She was the first child. My mother's [younger] children and Amy's children fight all the time. My mother would tell Amy how bad her children were, and Amy would say how she didn't like us [Elizabeth, her brothers, and her sisters] taking it out on her kids.

My mother would say how bad they were, and we were not to hang around with them. Amy would tell her kids this and her kids would resent us for that.

When Donny found out you were pregnant, did he want to get married?

I guess so. His parents told us that he should marry me. This I remember. They did tell me, whether he married me or not that he would support the baby. I ended up living with my mother, and my mother ended up taking over my son.

When we got married I really never knew where Donny was. I mean he would tell me he was gonna go to the store to pick up something for supper or something. He'd go, but he'd never return. The cupboard would be bare and the baby would be crying. There would be no milk or nothing, and it would be getting late, around eight or nine o'clock, and there would be nothing there. This would happen often. On pay days he would just disappear. One time some woman told me that she knew where he was, and if I wanted her to go with me, she'd go with me, and we walked down to this place called Billy's Bar. I looked in the window, and I saw him dancing with a woman with blond hair. He was rubbing her neck and stuff like that. I opened up the door quickly and said, "Donny," to let him know I saw him, and I started going out up the street. He started coming after me.

"It's not what you think. It's not . . . she's a friend of my father's. She's a friend of my father's." I said, "Yeah."

All the times he'd go, he was going out and getting drunk. He would come home sometimes two or three in the morning. One time he came home, and his shirt was off and there was a shoe missing and everything. You know. And so after that happened, the next couple of times he went out, I wouldn't let him in. I locked the door, and he banged on that door. I remember one time he was standing in the hallway, half froze to death, and I wouldn't let him in 'cause he used to come in and hit me. I didn't believe it. I didn't believe it. So anyway, finally about a year or so later I left him.

That's when you went to live with your mother?

She used to tell me to go and do this and do that, and that I was too young to raise a child. She still has my son today. He lives with her. We just started being close just this year. He's reaching out to me, because he would come over and kiss me good-bye and give me a hug.

Did he always know that you're his mother?

Yeah. My mother won't . . . I always resented the fact that she took him. I didn't like myself too well at first, but I felt this is what my mother wanted. And I thought by doing what my mother wanted, she would love me more, you know, and care about me. So when she said something about the baby, I would let her be that way, thinking she would care more about me.

I was always trying to do things. . . . If I did something she thought I should do, I thought she would care more about me.

So you took your son and went back to living with your mother. Did you go to work?

Yes, I did. Different odd jobs. They put me in a training program, and then they had me work with crippled children. That job I think I enjoyed the most of all, working with those kids. I knew that they didn't have very long to live like other children do, so I kind of enjoyed being around them and making them laugh. I worked there I think almost a year.

How old were you at that time?

Yeah, around twenty-one.

How did you meet Brad?

He was a dancer. He taught me how to dance, and I just loved that. We even performed in night clubs together. I loved being up there in front of those people.

I think I really loved Brad, but after we got married I think jealousy set in. I think he was jealous. He stopped me from my dancing. He wanted me to stay home. That was fine for a while. I stayed home. Then he got so he wasn't coming home. We ended up fighting after a while. He made me so I feared him. I felt, I had feelings. . . . I mean, he made me shake so much after a while that I just didn't dare stay with him. I wanted to stay with him, but I didn't dare. I was afraid.

Do you remember the first time he ever hit you?

I think we were on our honeymoon.

Do you remember anything that happened to lead to this?

I can't remember but I think the first time he just grabbed me, you know, put me up against the wall, and just started slapping me. I just shut right up. Didn't say nothing. Didn't do nothing. I was afraid of what he would do.

Like what?

Like for instance there was one time when Carol [her daughter] was crying and he got so mad that he just pushed her head into the counter. I got mad and I screamed at him, you know, "Leave her alone." He said, "She never shuts up."

Then there was another incident when she was eating her cereal. I was feeding her cereal. She was only about nine months old. She was in her high chair, and I was feeding her cereal. I had to go to the bathroom, something like that, and I asked him to finish feeding her. When I came out of the bathroom, he got mad at her for something, and he pushed the bowl of cereal right in her hair. I don't know why he got mad at her. I don't know what made him do that at that instant, but he did do that, unless he was trying to make me mad or something.

Did he ever hit her?

Yes. There were a few times that she was just walking and he picked her up and heaved her from one side of the room to another. To make me behave.

That used to scare me when he did that, but I couldn't understand it. I couldn't understand it. I didn't like staying there, and I didn't know how or why I did it.

How did his hitting you make you feel?

There was another time when he had taken me into the kitchen and said, "Now I'm gonna hit you." He wanted me to strike back. I never would strike back at him. I was too afraid. Afraid he would break my wrist. So, I wouldn't strike back for nothing. I didn't want to hit him. I couldn't understand why he wanted to hit me, but I didn't want to hit him.

So he hit me, and he said, "Now you are going to hit me." I said, "No, I'm not going to hit you. I don't want to hit you." I said, "Please just leave me alone." I started crying. He did it again, and I still didn't hit back. Then he just chuckled and walked off. . . .

How did that make you feel—when he laughed?

I wanted to kill him, but I didn't. I just said, "Why, why is this happening to me?" It was like he wanted to punish me.

Was he drunk when he did that?

Not that time. I don't think he was drinking at home. But it was like he wanted to punish me. There was another time when he kicked me. He just kept kicking me.

Did you feel angry?

Yeah, but I couldn't show it.

Do you know why?

I was too afraid. I don't think I felt . . . I never felt like I could strike him. I don't know if I ever could. I just didn't know how to give it back. Just couldn't do it.

I'm afraid of what I would do if I did. Even like when I got mad at the children and found myself pushing them aside because of what was going on with me. I was afraid to ever strike them because I might take it out on them for what I was going through. It wasn't their fault, I know, but at the time if I was that mad at him, and they did something, I wouldn't dare go to spank them. I'd send them to their room or something. I wouldn't spank them because I was afraid I would over-do it.

Did you ever think Brad would hurt Carol?

Yeah. Oh, yeah. I thought one time that he was trying to smother her with a pillow. I thought he was trying to kill her. Really kill her. You know, stop her from breathing. I thought if he would have killed her, I would have screamed or done something. And I did start doing something, or trying to do something about the way he was reacting with her. I think that afterwards was when he started hitting me. He didn't hit me before that. When I started standing up for my children, when I thought he was abusing Carol, he started hitting me. Carol is not really his, you know.

Did he know that?

Oh, yes. When he married me, Carol was a week old. But, he's the only father she has ever known. She won't call him father because of what's happened, but it's the only man that she ever knew.

After your other son came along, did he do the same things to him? Treating him rough like that?

No, no. I think that he was treating him okay. Since I left him, he comes around, tries to see the kids. Why he did that to Carol I don't know. He doesn't harm her physically like he did.

How long were you with Brad?

Well, I'd say about four and a half years.

When did you make the decision to leave?

I left quite a few times, but I kept going back. When I left him I was staying at my brother's house, and I didn't have any family doctor, and I called up Doctor Griffin. When I got there, I was sitting in a chair, and the nurse came in and asked if I could get up and walk around for a couple of minutes, and I told her that I felt dizzy. The last thing I remember is that I stood up and I passed out or something. When I came to, there was nurses around me and I went out again. Then when I came to again, nobody was in the room except the girl in the next bed. She said to me, "You've been out for a long time." Doctor Griffin told me that I was mentally exhausted.

What did Brad do when he found out that you were in the hospital?

He was trying to get into the hospital, and I didn't want to see him at all. Doctor Griffin left orders that if he tried to come into the hospital, that they wouldn't let him.

What was it like right before that time you left?

He was searching for me everywhere. Every time I left, he would search for me and find me. So I'd try it a different way. Then he would try to get me back.

And then you did go back?

I think I felt awful sorry for him. Then when I went back, I felt uneasy. He would be extra good to me for two weeks or a few days. As a matter of fact, sometimes he would wait on me hand and foot. If I didn't feel well or something, he would cook supper.

And then what would happen?

Then the baby would start fussing, and then he would start in again, and he would end up doing something like staying away from the house or not come home 'til the early hours of the morning. The minute I'd say something to him, he'd get angry and start pushing things around and slamming things down. At that point I'd shake like a leaf, and I'd just wish there was a way out.

Sometimes I'd wait until he'd go to sleep and to make sure that he was sleeping before I'd dare do anything. I knew I had to leave.

Did you ever call the police?

One time, yes, when I lived in the village I called the police. He was outside the house when they came. They took him for a walk around the block. That was the only time that I called the police.

Did you talk to this Doctor Griffin about him?

Yeah. Doctor Grifffin gave me some kind of pills. I don't know what they were, but I figure it was some kind of tranquilizer. The day after I took a couple of them pills was when I went into the hospital.

How long did you stay there?

I think it was a week.

Just in the regular hospital?

Yeah. But I know that I was . . . I thought I was going cripple. I felt like I couldn't get up and walk. I felt like I didn't have any legs to walk on.

How long did you take tranquilizers?

I took Valium back then for quite a while I think, about eight or nine months.

When you went over to the hospital, what did you go for?

I went to see, I don't know, the health doctor, the mental health doctor there.

You just felt ill?

Yeah. And physically, the pains in my legs were bad and, you know, they felt wobbly and weak and really pained me. And I was shaking so much and I really didn't know what was wrong, whether it was mentally or physically, but I knew I needed some kind of help.

You were in the hospital for a week and then you came out? Whose house did you go to then?

I went to my mother's house.

Did you ever go back to live with Brad after that?

I don't remember if I went back to Brad another time after that or not. I was back and forth so much at that time.

So you made the decision to get a divorce?

I went and had my tubes cut and tied, right after I had my mental, what I call my mental exhaustion, but the reason for me to have my tubes cut and tied in the first place was I didn't know whether I was gonna stay with Brad or not, and if I was, I didn't want . . . I wanted to make sure that I could never have any more children to bring into the kind of life I was living with him.

Was he making sexual demands on you?

Sometimes he was forcing me to do things I didn't want to do. And I thought that. . . . All I could think of when he tried to force sex on me or certain things that he would try to force me to do, and bothered me in bed was. . . . I can picture him laughing at me when he was trying to make me do these stupid things, and I'd look at him like he was this . . . this type of thing, you know. It was like with them guys. Even today if I go out on the street, it bothers me to go out on the street, especially if I see a gang of guys hanging around. I try not to go in that direction. I go the long way around. I'm afraid that . . . you know, sometimes I think one of them guys could be one of them guys that were there, because I don't remember who they were, and I'm always thinking that one of them guys could be in that gang or they're laughing at me. I go the other way.

Did Brad know about that experience you had as a teenager?

I don't remember exactly, but I don't think that I ever told Brad about those guys. No, I don't think so.

You never tried to make him understand?

No. No, but this husband I'm married to now, I did tell him, and he still keeps after me about some things he wants me to do, that I don't want to do. He keeps asking me to do it and do it and do it. I wish I could tell him, "Just leave me alone, and don't ask me to do that." I don't think that I can have a normal relationship with a man, no matter how they are, because of this type of thing that has happened to me, because when I can, because no matter how much I care about it, I can seriously feel hatred toward them if they try to get me to do certain things that I don't want to do. At that time I hate them. Really, they're better off leaving me alone. Even if they ask me nicely. Especially if they know I don't want to. And especially if they keep asking me every night or something, and they keep at me and keep at me, and then they make me feel that . . . well, I'm not good enough for them. I'm not woman enough for them. Then I say to myself, "Well, if you're not content with me the way I am, just go find somebody else," you know. This is what I'm feeling inside. Or I tell them [all three husbands] sometimes, you know, if you're not content with me. . . . This is what I told my husband that I'm married to now, find something else, because I cannot do this kind of thing, and I wish you'd stop asking me to.

So you did tell somebody about your experience with those guys?

Today, I mean like right now, I can talk about it. I mean I feel a little bit uneasy down inside talking about it, but it's okay.

I felt I could talk to Bruce [the third husband] a little bit. I had to get it out. Now it's him. I told him about the guys, but I couldn't say what happened to me when I was a child. How could you say that to a man you're married to? No, I couldn't say anything.

Tell me about your present marriage?

Bruce has been pretty good with the children. That's one thing I can say for him. I don't know why. But Brad was different. I would think he was molesting Carol.

Sexually?

Yeah. That's when I knew I had to get away from him. I don't know if it was true or not, but I couldn't say anything. I just remembered what happened to me when I was a child.

There was another man in my life, but my mother and father didn't want me to go with him. They stopped me from seeing him. Brad and I had separated or divorced. I had been on my own, and Timmy was my old friend. I thought all my life that I really wanted to be with him, but mother . . . [my] parents said I shouldn't be with him, but he was one guy I thought I could spend the rest of my life with and be with and love him, because he didn't want me to do things.

I didn't want to go against my parents' wishes. They were old-fashioned. You see, Timmy, he was crooked. This is why they didn't like him. But he never hit me, never tried to make me. . . .

What happened then?

Then my father died, and after my father died, I moved up on a lake in a cottage with Timmy. Timmy had got into trouble, I guess. After I had moved all my stuff up there, Timmy hadn't shown up at the cottage. I had no food. I had no phone, no sense of direction around there. I couldn't get around town with no car. My family had never been up there. They didn't try to get me. I didn't know how to get a-hold of anybody, and I just set up there right outside my door waiting and wondering where he was, and if he's coming back. So finally one day this woman came out and got me to a phone and I reached somebody and gave some directions for them to come and get me. By the time I got back up there to get my stuff, the place was in a shambles, and all my stuff had been taken out of there. My dishes and food and stuff, gone. Girls' nightgowns were all over like they were having a party.

Did you ever see him again?

No. After that I didn't see Timmy again. I don't know what happened to him or where he went or nothing.

Then Bruce came along. He seemed more mature, or older, and I don't know, he make me feel. . . . I needed some type of security. He wanted to get married too.

Did you love him?

I thought a lot of Bruce, but I don't think I really loved him. I knew that he had a lot of feelings for me at times. I thought he really loved me, but I don't . . . I think I just wanted a family for my children, and I thought that he would be good for that. Where if I

married someone that loved me and not someone that I knew would
hurt me more, I thought that maybe I could lead some type of normal
life with him.

Then, what happened?

After we got married . . . well, when we got married, well . . . I
didn't spend our wedding day together. For three days I wandered
around the streets crying. It all started the day I got married. It didn't
happen before. Everything was just so nice and the children were there
and everything. It all started the day I got married. The day of our
wedding he got drunk. When we got married, he was drunk. He was
hollering it out loud while the minister was performing the services. I
kept thinking I'm being made a fool of.

What did you do?

I couldn't speak back. Maybe because I couldn't speak back to my
brother when he took advantage of me like that. I couldn't speak back
at the time, because I didn't know how. When I speak back I don't want
to hurt nobody else. I know at the time that I'd hurt myself first, before
I'd hurt somebody else. This is why I've gone through a lot of hurt,
because I hurt myself before I hurt others. Just like the kids being in a
home. I don't want to hurt them, but at the same time I'm hurting
myself, but at the same time I'm trying to help them the best way I
know how. I can't explain that.

You miss the kids?

Sure. And I don't know to this time whether it really . . . I mean,
I think it's the right thing, but then sometimes I wonder if it really is or
what? I don't want them to. . . . I never want them to think that I
don't care. I never believed anybody really cared, that's why.

In the eight or nine months you've been with Bruce, has he hit you?

He hasn't really, really hit me. He's shoved me around, pushed me
a little bit, shoved me, but that's all he has to do. I'd feel the reaction to
when I was beaten before, or think he was going to . . . I start shaking
real bad like I did before when I was getting hit. I think it's worse than
when they hit you. When you think they're going to, and when they
really do it. I think I'd rather have them hauling off and hit you than act
like he was going to, not know what he was gonna do.

When did you come to the shelter the first time?

The first time I came to the shelter? Well, I was referred to the
shelter by an extension worker at the state office. That was on Monday.
The state office was closed, and I was ready to just . . . I didn't want
to go back home. I wanted to do something with the kids, so I called my
state worker, and asked her. They referred me to the shelter.

What did you think about during the time you were at the shelter?

When I was first there, I was in a daze. I was scared all the time. I felt helpless. I don't know what was happening to me. At the time, I just couldn't stand my kids with me. I loved them, but I just couldn't cope with them around me at the time. I felt like putting my fist through something or jumping out a window or . . . quitting. So many times up there . . . and eventually after talking to someone or trying to do something, I find that my feelings have changed quickly to so much better that I don't do anything to myself. But there are moments when I do feel that it keeps coming back. At the time I think that I just need someone to talk with, and then I feel all right.

Then you just disappeared?

I started feeling like, I can't give up. I don't want to leave my home again. I've lost it so many times before, and this is the first time I have left Bruce. Maybe by my staying away like I have been so many days [at the shelter], maybe if I go back he'll realize that things are getting better. You know, and I'll give it a second try, and this is what I did.

What happened after you went back to Bruce?

We kept having a lot of fights that we never had before, because of the way he was trying to keep at me about sexual things, and I got back there the second time.

I found that I had to leave again. I stayed there for almost a week after I decided to leave again, and then one day the children left for school, and I said when they come home from school, I'll pack up the children and go.

I think that so many pressures came upon me between coming back and finding out that he had been with his exwife when I was gone. I felt I couldn't stay there because she was around there all the time when I was gone.

You decided to leave again?

I called the shelter and somebody answered, but I can't remember who it was, and I said I used to be in the shelter before, and would it be all right if I came down. She said, "Sure, come on down." So I went.

What did you feel when you came back to the shelter?

When I first came to the shelter I felt happy. When I came up those stairs, and it was like a big reunion, I was so happy, because it was like a good feeling. And when I sat down, I really didn't have any feeling of trying to do this, or trying to do that. I guess I just wanted someone to talk to. You know? I hurt, but then after I got finished talking I felt better.

What do you think you're going to do now?

I really don't know what I'm gonna do now, or what's gonna happen. I know I want to try to get relief somehow. I know I need someone to talk to. I can feel real good at night and then it can change so completely. When the nightfall comes, I am gone. I can't stand it, but I'm trying to deal with it. I just call myself an ordinary individual person.

CHAPTER 6

Paula

At 31 Paula fled from her home with her two children. She had been abused for 10 years. She had headaches every day and almost constant colitis.

Paula's history illustrates may of the research findings on the social structural characteristics of battered women. Both she and her husband came from abusive homes. Their marital relationship was male-dominated. Paula was isolated from other sources of financial and emotional support, and neither she nor her husband had strong social support systems, especially from family networks.

When Paula came to the shelter, she talked about her fantasies of murdering her husband. Some battered women eventually do murder their husbands, so Paula's fantasies of murder were taken seriously.

Paula did not murder her husband, however. She is now living alone with her children. She has a job and is free from the routine of drugs prescribed for her physical and psychological symptoms.

Paula's story was told to Mary Price (the former director of the shelter) and me in the sparsely furnished apartment where she lived six months after her stay in the shelter. Identifying details have been changed to protect her and her family. Her life history provides insight into what brought Paula to the point of thinking she might kill her husband, Ed, and also what may have stopped the pattern of escalating violence that could have led her to kill him.

PAULA'S LIFE HISTORY

Paula, how did you meet Ed?

I was living in the city and going with another guy when I met Ed. I had a date with this other guy 'cause we were going to go apartment hunting. He stood me up, so I decided I was gonna go eat. That's always been my thing—when I'm upset, I eat. So I went down to a pizza house. That's where I met him, at the pizza house.

How old were you?

Twenty-one, and he was eighteen. Yeah. In fact his father threatened before we got married that he was going to put me in jail for robbing the cradle.

How long did you go with him before you got married?

Three months. Well in the three months before we got married, I got pregnant and lost a child. Right after I lost the child was when we got married.

When you got pregnant during those three months. . . . What happened?

Well, Ed was always throwing me up in the air, tossing me around, and wrestling and. . . .

Before you got married?

Yeah. We lived together those three months and he was always being rough, very rough.

You didn't consider it violent?

No. He was just very rough and I guess that's what did it, 'cause he was always picking me up and putting me on his shoulders. He was playing around. I just took it being . . . I didn't know I was pregnant. But right after, I started hemorrhaging. I started slowly. I started bleeding and I went to a doctor and he gave me some pills or something and then I really started.

And then you got married?

Yeah. I panicked, because I thought, "Oh, I can never have another child." Felt so depressed, so very down. And I think he married me out of feeling sorry because I was so depressed.

I think my mother had a lot to do with it too. When I was twenty, my mother told me that "after you've been with every Tom, Dick, and Harry, nobody's going to have you anyway." I know the first one that said anything about getting married, I was all for it, because she said no one would want me.

I don't think I really loved him, because I only knew him three months. I think it's just because he said let's get married. You know, and I said, ah, this is an answer, "Somebody wants me."

You were married three months and then he enlisted?

I enlisted him. Yeah, 'cause we fought the whole three months that we were married. He was calling me names and downing me, and I was kind of in a panic situation without knowing what to do about it.

He hadn't been in the service yet, and he was worried about getting drafted, so I called up the draft board and said more or less, "Come and get him." I called the Marine Corps, and I said, "My husband is interested in joining the Marine Corps; would you come and talk to him?" I felt he was going to get drafted anyway.

That was when he went to Vietnam?

No. First he went to boot camp, then he went for special weapons training. Meanwhile I got pregnant again. In fact, the day he was leaving for Vietnam I had Denise.

Really?

Yeah. He called me on the phone. He used to call me every Sunday when I was pregnant. I lived with his parents for about six months after I got pregnant and then there was a big fight and I left and went to live with my girl friend.

His family didn't speak English. Oh, the two brothers did speak English, but they wouldn't translate for me. I felt isolated and . . . with nothing to do.

His sister had also started threatening she was going to kill me and cut my throat and the whole bit. The whole family is very violent. When she got mad, the first thing she could think of was kill. So I said, "I'm not going to stay here and have her walk up beside me sometime and belt me beside the head with a crowbar or something." It don't bother them any to shoot anybody. So that's when I went to live with my girl friend. He used to call me every Sunday, and one Sunday he called and I wasn't there. I was in the hospital. I was in the delivery room. He called the hospital and said that he was on the way to Vietnam. And I said, "Well, you have a daughter." He was very excited about it.

How did you feel?

I felt very depressed, very lonely, having a baby by myself. To me, the husband is supposed to be there. I was very scared knowing he wasn't going to be there. I'd never had a baby before.

After you had Denise, did you go back to your girl friend's house?

No. Yes, for three weeks 'cause I wasn't allowed to travel. Then I moved in with my mother. But I didn't stay very long. No. I discovered that the reason that I left home before was that my mother and I didn't get along. So after I got on my feet, I started looking for a job and an apartment and I got both.

And then what happened?

I was out working, and the other people used to go out drinking and having a good time, and they finally talked me into going out with them. So I started drinking and the first thing you want to do when you start drinking is go out looking for men, and that's what I did. I met this one man who was a truck driver and he was very nice. He wanted to take me out, show me a good time, spend money on me. Who could say no? I didn't.

That went on for quite a while as I recall.

Yeah, for about a month before Ed returned, then I got really scared. I was dreading Ed coming home. It scared me to think that somebody had seen me out and would recognize me and come over and say "Hi" to me because Ed was very jealous. Very possessive.

What kinds of things did you write back and forth when Ed was in Vietnam? What did he write to you? What did you write to him?

Oh, how dull life was—how I was staying home every night and working very hard and all that situation here.

I wondered if he was writing you about what was going on with him at all?

Even to this day he has told me nothing. Just that it was very rough. It was very bad. As far as going into detail, he has told me nothing.

You were married and had a child, but did you really know each other?

We did not know anything about each other. The first three months of marriage—or the first six months, 'cause we were living together three months—we spent in bed. Seven, eight times a day. That's all he wanted to do. We didn't have time to eat. We didn't have time to do nothing. That was his whole life, sex. He just couldn't get enough. He was possessed by it. It was really dominant in his life.

So then he came back?

Yeah. The first night he came back I expected all this loving and kissing and everything, right, you know, but it wasn't. He came back and he stuck a knife up to my throat, he threatened to kill me.

I was going across the hall to a next-door neighbor's when I saw him down at the bottom of the stairs. I knew he was coming, but I didn't know when. I saw him at the bottom of the stairs, and he ran up the stairs and kissed me, and hugged me. We went in the house and he said, "What were you going next door for?" I said, "I was just going over there to talk to the neighbors." This was what started it . . . walking across the hall to talk to the neighbors.

Tell me exactly what happened next?

He was talking and all of sudden he walloped me. "Who you been out with?" I said, "Nobody." He said, "Don't lie to me," and I said, "I haven't been out with anybody." He just kept going on and on. "Yes, you have. I know you have." He didn't believe me. He was really crazy.

He threatened to kill me. I should have known right then and there—you've got to get out of here. He was really evil looking and crazy. That's when he started unpacking and he whipped out this knife. He just went berserk. He was like you see on TV—these guys with the knives. They throw the knives back and forth from hand to hand. He was doing that. All this time he was screaming at me, and hollering at me, and threatening me.

So how did it stop?

I guess my crying . . . screaming back at him. I really got so upset I was shaking. He found out that I was scared. I finally admitted that I had gone out with one guy, and only one. Then he kind of sat down and talked about it. He calmed down.

Then the next day, something happened with Denise?

Yes. The next day he was taking a shower and he wanted to take Denise in with him. She was only fifteen months old. He took her and put her face right up to the shower head. He swore, "Whose kid is this anyway?" He didn't even believe she was his. She looks just like him.

He thought it was funny. He said, "I'm just playing with her." He doesn't know half the time the things he's doing. Like when he did something to one of the kids, and I said, "Ed, don't do that." He'd say, "I didn't do anything." Sometimes it makes me wonder whether he has memory lapses or something like that.

Did you have the feeling that going to Vietnam had changed him?

Yes. He saw a lot of kids get . . . what I could get out of it, he had seen a lot of kids that were used by the Vietnamese to trap the soldiers. Hand grenades under their arms, that type of thing.

And he loves children, at least I think he does. I really don't know what . . . I can't tell what's inside him. Sometimes he can be violent and other times he can be very loving and kind.

He's never told anybody about it.

So he came back when you were living in the apartment? Then did you stay in that apartment or. . . .

We had about six or eight apartments right after he came back. They were all within walking distance of his friends.

It was all right for a while, but he fought a lot with his family. At one time, we lived in the same apartment house as his sister. She lived downstairs, we lived upstairs, and he had a fistfight with his sister.

This is the one that had threatened to kill you?

Yeah. In fact, for a while he didn't even talk to his parents after this fistfight with his sister. It was four years. We lived in the same city, right around the block, and he never once spoke to his parents or his sister for four years.

After that real blow-up after he first came home, how long was it before you got into another thing?

I really don't know. My sister came to stay with us. Ed had lost his temper about something and he started to hit me. My sister tried to defend me, tried to help me, and he belted her. And then he just kept hitting me, over, and over, and over, and over. He slapped me in the face as hard as he could. He never used his fist, but he slapped me in the face. He was very strong and, to me, it felt like his fist.

I kicked him out and I called the cops. They came in and walked around the house and said, "Well, he's not here." I said, "No, of course not. He ran away when he heard me calling the cops." They looked around and saw all his Marine Corps things on the walls and they said, "Well, if he's a Marine, he can't be all that bad." And out they walked. They said, "We'll keep an eye out for him and if we see him, we'll grab him." And that was all that was done. Back at the time, if I had gone down and signed a restraining order . . . but it cost $25 and I didn't have any money, so he was out for two weeks, and then he came back crawling, you know, every day, "I'm sorry." How it would never happen again.

Then, when I was seven or eight months pregnant with Danny, he beat me up again. I say beat me when he just slaps me with his hand. He makes my face all swell up black and blue, but he doesn't punch me. He kept slapping me, and slapping me, and slapping me, so I went down to the state hospital after he went to work to find out whether there was anything I could do. This man keeps beating me up, you know, what can I do about it?

The place wouldn't do anything about it. They said it took three psychiatrists to commit him. I said, "He has to be crazy if he keeps beating up on a pregnant woman." They wouldn't do anything. They said, "Well, you could come in for counseling." So we went—twice I think it was, and he wouldn't go back again. He wouldn't go back again. I kept telling him, "You know, there's got to be something wrong with you if you have to keep slapping me around." "Well," he says, "I'll go get help if you want me to, but these guys don't know anything."

So he went down to the military hospital. They asked him to stay and get treatment. He said, "F— you," and out he went.

Was he drinking, Paula?

No. He doesn't drink. He doesn't take drugs either. He doesn't do any of that. He just keeps having this uncontrollable temper. He can't control it.

So he walked out of there when they wanted to treat him?

Yeah. He said, "They wanted to keep me and they ain't keeping me. I ain't gonna be locked up in no hospital."

You were willing to go yourself in order to? . . .

Yeah. But nobody's willing to help us. If you're not on welfare and you haven't got the money, they're not gonna help you.

He was working at this point?

He was away a lot after work, but most of the time he said he was visiting with his boyfriends there, and all those men he liked to hang around with. He would spend all his time with them. Whether he had another girl, or not, I don't know.

Was he still hitting you at this time?

Yeah. He'd lose his temper and he'd just belt me. Shut me out. It was mostly the beating of the head or mouth that really tore me apart. When he called me names and said how stupid I was and how ugly I looked. So much fat. How he'd tell me how I couldn't do anything with my life 'cause I was too stupid.

Did he do that only when he was mad or did he do that a lot of the time?

He did that a lot. He called me a bitch. I don't know why. It makes me angry. It really bothered me. But you know, five minutes later, after being called all these names, telling me how stupid, fat, and ugly I was, he'd want me to get into bed with him. That's what messed up my mind the worst. How he could get over it so fast and here I would dwell on it for six months.

How did that make you feel?

I wouldn't feel anything. I would say, out of ten years of our marriage, I would feel like maybe a week's worth. I just wouldn't feel like it, you know, 'cause like after somebody telling you off and hollering and screaming at you and telling . . . and then want to make love with you. I'd fake it just so that he wouldn't continue screaming, continue hollering. I'd just go to bed with him and fake it. It got so I didn't know whether I was faking or what. I didn't know what I was feeling or when I was feeling or what. It would go on like months, and months, and months, and months when I'd be depressed.

What did you do when you were depressed?

I'd keep low. I didn't want to do anything and I didn't want to go anywhere. I didn't want to visit anybody. Especially when he was around I was more depressed than ever. I didn't want to do anything that would make him angry. I was like a robot. I didn't feel anything. I didn't want to feel anything.

Was there ever "I love you" discussion after these incidents?

Oh, "I love you" all the time, enough to make you sick. But, I didn't believe half the things he told me, like when he said he loved me. Because to me, anybody that pounds somebody one minute and then says "I love you" the next is not telling the truth. I mean, how can anyone love somebody and still beat on them? Or even call them dirty names and swear at them. It's not my idea of a relationship that you have to be browbeaten—having someone say "I love you" to make it all better. Maybe that's why I went out with other men . . . to try to find the real type of love, which I didn't find.

Did you feel guilty about that?

I don't know what. I would today if I did, but then . . . no, I never did. It didn't bother me as far as my relationship with him goes, because to me I didn't have one.

You left at one point in there, didn't you?

Yeah. We lived in the city for a year, and he discovered that he couldn't handle the financial load and he wanted me to go to work. Danny was just three. I didn't want to go to work until Danny went to school full-time because I would just be working to pay the baby-sitter. I told him that. I said, "I'm not going to work until Danny goes to school full-time," and we had a big scene. You know, swearing and hollering, the whole bit. "You lazy bitch. You're going to work whether you want to or not," and "You're gonna do what I want you to do." There was this whole big scene about I'd go to work or I'd be dead. There was no way out of it. I had to do what he told me to do.

I had my own car at the time. It was the family car, but it was in my name. One day I packed up the car with the Christmas presents and everything—the cat, the dog, the kids, and took off.

Where did you go?

I went to my mother's. We spent Christmas there, but I had . . . I had a rough time. She was hassling me about Danny, always downing him to me. I felt protective because she was always downing him. I think that has a lot to do with Danny taking to look so much like Ed and acting like him. He's working his way out of this now, but still he gets in an argument on the street and he comes home screaming and hollering and stamping his feet. Slamming doors, telling how he's going to beat up on some kid. He's got a very violent temper and he loses it very easily.

I had Christmas dinner at my sister's. I had, well I'd say, a little bit of a nervous upset. We were sitting at the table, and my sister, my little sister, my baby sister joked around. Really comical, and I laughed so much that I couldn't stop laughing. I turned blue 'cause I couldn't catch my breath. I really scared my mother. Really panicked her so she said I had to go have my heart checked. It was just nerves.

Did anybody in your family know that he was hitting you?

I would never tell anybody. Well, like I talked to some of my friends once in a while but. . . . My parents did know because they'd seen a couple of times. In fact, he slapped me before we even got married, so they knew. Even though I didn't tell at first, when I started running home every year or so, they began to. . . .

See, this is my biggest problem. I suppress everything. And I just can't . . . I can't express my feelings no matter how hard I try. I can't do it. It's all inside. I don't know how I feel. And I have a lot now, like that gnawed feeling type situation. Even now I can't cry.

How long have you had that kind of feeling?

As long as I can remember.

It's not . . . not just since you've been abused?

No. I was abused as a child too. Not a lot. But my father, when he spanked me, he did so severely. I didn't remember it myself, but my mother told me that the beatings were so bad that I was black and blue. She didn't want us kids around, because they fought constantly. He drank. He was an alcoholic, and she didn't have any use for us at that time. I can remember it in my head that all our lives she told us how she hated kids. How we were all mistakes and we always were in her way, and she could never go to work and get a job. She could have never left my father because she had three kids. That has a lot to do with my problems today. I feel like I've never really ever, ever loved Ed because I don't know if I can give love. It has a lot to do with me not being able to show love. I can't do it. Sure, I can hug and kiss my kids, but I really don't—you know, I just don't feel like it. It doesn't come easy. I have to force myself to do it. And I do it because of them.

It is people who have been abused who tend to repeat the pattern with their own kids.

I think that is Ed in a nutshell, because he was badly abused as a child, but he won't talk about it. He won't even . . . he had a very bad childhood. It's just what his mother did, so he's going on the way his mother beat. He's just repeating it, doing it to his own child.

How much abuse was there with the kids?

He was always telling Denise, "You fat pig! Cow! Horse!!" because she's awkward. You know, she's not graceful like a little girl's supposed to be. She's awkward and she's tomboyish. He said to me lately, when we've been able to talk to each other without any arguments getting into it, that there's something about Denise that irritates him. He doesn't know whether she reminds him of somebody. . . .

You told me one time that she looks like his sister?

It's very possible that she reminds him of his sister. There's something that—it's almost like it rubs on him. He just . . . he tries. He comes down and hugs and kisses her but he . . . you know. She can't respond to him and he expects her to. He expects her to want to kiss him, but she don't want to.

I used to leave them alone a lot so they could develop their own relationship, and later things would come out that he'd thrown her up against the wall or he'd—he was always taking his knuckles and hitting them. Cracking them in the head with them. You know? "Shut up. Don't do that." He would not allow them to talk when they were watching TV. They were not allowed to talk when they were eating. There was no friendliness. To me, when you sit down at the table, everybody talks and has a good time. But to him, you got to be quiet. You're not allowed to talk. You're not allowed to do nothing. You got to eat fast. . . .

It's almost like you were a bystander. You were watching it all happen.

Like I was gone two years.

You also were not in touch with a lot of other feelings?

I had to learn not to feel. All these things that I would watch him do, or all these things he would do to me . . . I would have to kind of get inside myself and just not feel anything. You know? I tried to talk to him about hitting the kids in the head and he promised he wouldn't do it again, and he would do it again the next time he got angry. He'd come home angry. He'd wake up angry. It was just like my mother used to say, "He had a twenty-four-hour mad-on." All the time he was angry. He was mad all the time.

He went to a doctor after one of the times he hit me. He didn't want to, but I said, "Either go and get help or this is it. This is the end of it. I'm gonna leave and I'm not gonna come back." So he went to the doctor and had all kinds of tests, and he went to a specialist, and they said he had muscle tension headaches.

I remember he had those incredible headaches, didn't he?

Yes, but all those years he didn't tell me about them. He wouldn't say that he had a headache. He'd have these headaches and then he'd get ugly. But he wouldn't tell me he had these headaches. The doctor gave him some pills to take, and he took them a couple of times and then he wouldn't take them any more. He hates taking medication.

Paula, what happened when you were at your mother's and you had that time when you choked up and everything. Then did you go back to your mother's, or did Ed come and get you? What happened?

Oh, I know what happened. Christmas Day I called him, because I thought for Christmas, he could come over for Christmastime. Plus living with my mother is enough to drive anybody back to. . . .

I called him and tried to talk to him and he started in to crying how he had been bad. How I wouldn't have to go to work, you know, all these promises, promises. Plus, living with my mother is enough to drive anybody back to . . . I said, "Well maybe one more time. We'll do it." And he was good for about a month and he'd lose his temper for some reason or something would happen at work, he'd come home and take it out on me.

What prompted you to move to the country?

His buddy talked him into building a house, saying how low farmer's home interest loans were and how you can get a house for $100 a month. I thought it would be a nice idea to go out into the country. The kids would have a nice place to play. But what I didn't realize was I never liked living in the country as a kid myself. I just didn't stop to think of that. Oh good, brand new house, you know? Who would want to pass this up? Well, I mean, I just went along with it. I thought it would be neat—a change of scenery, kids would have a place to quiet down, and go to school on the bus. I didn't stop to think there wouldn't be any kids in the area, in the neighborhood, to play with.

And you all moved?

Yes. We moved there and I started going to church in April. Oh, I was isolated. Oh—it was terrible. Like being caged.

He was going to work every day and he'd come home. . . . He started coming home right after work at 4:30. Then it got later, five o'clock, six o'clock. Sometimes he wouldn't come home until seven o'clock. I said, "Well, what were you doing?" He said, "I had things to do, people to see." And I was alone. No car, no way to get anywhere except my bicycle. Two miles to the nearest store. No entertainment. Nothing.

Was there anybody that you could talk to about what was going on?

There was one girl friend down the road from me, Sheila, that started me going to church. I went to her a lot because she was . . . would be around. She had three children. She had been an abused wife, and I talked to her a lot because we could communicate with the things that had happened to her. Of course, worse things happened to her than to me. He would actually not feed her. Not buy her groceries or anything. That kind of situation. She is the one that really helped me a lot—being able to talk to somebody that it had happened to, too. And she would always say, "I don't know why you stay." I didn't, you know, but I didn't have any way out. At least I thought I didn't. I stayed for something else, but I would go to her and tell her. Talk to her about it. And I would involve myself with the church so that I could keep my mind off what was going on at home. I had more things to do. Sometimes I would be going out three or four times a week to the church.

What did Ed think about it?

At first Ed didn't like it. He would come home and call me a "holy roller" and say how I was gone all the time. For a while he refused to let me have the car. So I'd go down to the end of the road and wait for one of the ladies going to the church to pick me up. I said, "I don't need your car. There's plenty of people who'll pick me up." After a while, when we were leaving him alone on Sunday morning, he got . . . he didn't like being alone on Sunday morning. Finally he started going and then everybody—oh, they said, oh, they were so happy to see him that they would just fall all over him. And he loved that. He loved all the attention. And it just fell into place. 'Course he wasn't behaving like he should at home, even though he was going to church on Sunday, and he just wouldn't, you know, commit himself.

I couldn't understand how he could go to church every week and come home and beat me up. It was . . . it was too much for my head. I just couldn't comprehend how somebody could say one thing and do something else all in the same breath practically. Then when he got swearing at me, and hollering at me, I said, "And you're supposed to be a Christian? You know, you've really messed up my life as far as Christianity was concerned." I'd committed my life, and I wanted to live a good life, and he would come home and start screaming and hollering. Often we'd have a fight before we'd go to church.

When you said you committed yourself, Paula, what did you mean exactly by that?

You know, just being a good husband or a good wife and doing what Christ wants you to do. That's why it was so hard for me to make the decision to do more. A husband and wife should work things out and make things out. Christ is supposed to give you the love that you need for each other. Something to pray about and work at. That's why it was so hard for me to make the break when we finally decided divorce was the only way. But talking to Sheila made me think. Why would Christ want anybody to live in such terror and such fear? Hell on earth really. She had a lot of insight as far as what Christ said. She reads the Bible supposedly every day. I haven't for a long time. Maybe that's part of my depression problem, because I don't read it. And I don't get out of these depressions.

But, Ed is reading every day. He says he's completely different from the way he was before, but as I said to the pastor, and I said to my new pastor here, I don't think even if he grows wings and has a halo, it will be enough. I mean he could be a preacher. He could be a new person, but I don't think he could make up for all the things he's done. No matter what he does. I think maybe I should try to make it work, but I don't feel it inside.

What do you mean?

I think on the outside. I think in my head that I should try it. 'Cause I should try to make it work. But I can't guarantee that I'm gonna stay. I just have the feeling that I'm a free person and I don't have to stay where I'm . . . where I don't want to be. And I don't think any man has the right to make me afraid. I never had that feeling until I went to the shelter. I thought I had to take it. I thought I had to sit there and take it because the church says you have to work things out.

Was it then that you went to the shelter?

No. I went into the hospital a few months before I came to the shelter. I was sick, physically sick. I had aches and pains in my joints which I thought was arthritis. I had headaches every single day. I went into the hospital to get help for my colitis. I was supposed to be out within a week, but they took all these tests and found nothing wrong with me. They kept taking more tests—they took every test in the book. At the end of two weeks they said, "There's nothing wrong with you. Physically and mentally, you're just worn out." So they kept me in two extra weeks for the rest. Then they put me on the Valium. They said it was my nerves. I was so nervous that it was causing all these other problems.

When I got out, Ed was still abusing me mentally and I got that attitude that I just didn't care. I think the Valium had a lot do with it. Nothing seemed to bother me. He would sit there and scream at me. I timed it. "Are you done now?" I'd ask him. It just didn't faze me a bit. It was like I was watching somebody else.

Then one night he came home very ugly. He had been coming home ugly for a week so I stayed away from him. He made me and the kids kiss him. Then he noticed something on the floor. He hit Denise in the head with his fist. He was shouting at her and she tried to avoid him.

He went down in the cellar to fix the stove and I went down to try to talk to him. He wanted me to bend over so he could have sex downstairs. I said, "I don't drop my pants every time you turn around and want sex." He said, "You do what I tell you to do." But I didn't! He wanted it always when the kids were around or, you know, that type of situation. I figured the place for such things was in the bedroom after the kids had gone to bed, and were asleep, not when they're off playing around, running in and out of the house. It didn't matter to him what time of day it was. I tried to open the stove and I opened it the wrong way. It was supposed to be a specially opened stove. I opened it the wrong way and he took his belt to me.

When we went back upstairs to eat, we were sitting at the table and he was saying something—"You're gonna . . ." do something. I said, "No, I don't want to," and he kicked me in the leg under the table. I said, "Don't kick me." He said, "I'll kick you if I want to. I'll do anything I want to you." Then he hit me with a stick and said I'd do anything he wanted me to because I was his property. That's when I decided I'm nobody's property. Just like I didn't care, you know. Who was he to tell me that I was his property?

What did you do after that?

I called my sister—Connie. She is the battered wife. Her husband used to drink. When he drank, he'd go crazy and beat her up. She was really beaten. I mean, she'd been beaten bad. But he's been off alcohol for a couple of years and they're both very . . . very much involved in their church. But he would go off church and go onto alcohol—beat her up, and then go back to church. Then he'd be the nice guy again. So I called her up and said, "Connie, what am I gonna do? I cannot take this mental abuse." It was mental abuse. It was mentally that he was abusing me, not physically. I just couldn't take all this . . . me feeling so numb inside and this feeling of panic. And this feeling of being caged—all at the same time. Panicked and caged, and not being able to go anywhere and do anything. It was like he was an animal trainer, coming and beating on the bars of the cage with a stick—only he was outside the bars so he couldn't get hurt.

Connie told me to call the police and ask them, 'cause she had seen something about battered women. I had too, but I thought it was out West. I didn't know there was anything here. That didn't enter my head. I said, "Okay," and hung up. I thought, no, I'll call Human Services because they would know more than the police would. I use the name "battered wife" because that's what they use on TV. "Battered wives." In fact, when I saw it, I had told Ed, "Come in and watch this with me. That's you and me on TV there." He just laughed about it. He thought it was funny. But it was true, you know.

You called about the shelter right after the incident in the cellar?

Yeah. The next day. 'Cause I kept thinking, you know, if he thinks he can do anything he wants, what would stop him from killing me?

I remember you told me that you thought that if you didn't get out of that situation you would kill him yourself. Remember that?

Yeah. I used to lay awake after he would beat me and then take me to bed, and think very angry thoughts of how I could get away with killing him and not get caught. Like there was a lot of shows on TV about wives killing their husbands with burning them up, and there was another one with icicles, you know—stabbing them with an icicle and then it would melt and there would be no. . . . I would just be so angry and kept saying, "I cannot live with this man. I hate him." But he won't leave and he won't let me leave, 'cause he would not allow me to leave. He said, "I'll kill you." And he said, "I'll take the kids and leave the country." He kept threatening me. I kept saying, "Ed, I can't take any more. I want out of here." He kept saying, "You're not going anywhere unless it's in a casket." So I would be so angry I would lay awake at night thinking, "There's got to be a way out. There's got to be some help somewhere." And then I'd go to sleep and it would have to be forgotten, because it was like being in a cage.

I can't deny my feeling of being trapped for the rest of my life. It was enough to make anybody go crazy. I just didn't know what to do.

What did you feel when you first came to the shelter?

When I came to the shelter, my first impression was safety. Nobody can hurt me here, nobody can get me. I went through a lot of phases in there. After feeling the safety, then there was having to get the kids back and forth to school. You know—wearing disguises. I was afraid to be out on the street because Ed worked in the city.

I guess there was a lot of fear involved in it. He could have been anywhere. Even though he wasn't out looking for me, and he had no idea where I was, to me there was just fear, still being afraid. Being seen by one of his friends that I didn't even know.

What other feelings did you have besides fear?

After the fear I went through the stage of being mad because he had *made* me afraid. You know, more like revengeful fearing. I wanted to get back at him for making me afraid. Who was he to have the right to make me afraid? After I realized that I was angry, I was mad, because he made me afraid and made my children afraid. They were just as scared, if not more, than I was. Being out, going back and forth to school, you know. And to think that he could do this to them, make them afraid of *him*, their own father, really made me even more angry. To the point that I'd have cut his throat if I'd got the chance. I don't know whether I'd have actually gone through with it, but I wanted to because he'd done this to all of us.

Then came the feeling of panic. I'm going to have to be on my own, look for an apartment, look for a job. I think that's mostly why . . . I was getting to the end of my three weeks of being at the shelter and I hadn't made a decision about whether I wanted to go home or not. I felt *guilty* for leaving, *guilty* for being angry, *guilty* for taking the kids away from their father, and on, and on, and on. Big long list of guilts. Why I should go back, why I should try it again. Not knowing what was right, what was wrong—still really not knowing now.

What's it been like the past few months?

Starting the divorce, separation, whatever—I don't know. I'm just doing what I feel. And then the pastor and Ed keep saying, "You can't live by feelings alone." If you don't live by feelings, what do you live by? I feel what I'm doing is right and that's the only way I can see it. I can't go any further than that.

Ed hadn't been coming around much until this past week, when I called him and decided to give it one more shot. I don't know. I asked him to come over for supper—it changes so quick. He wants . . . he's been begging me. Even when he came on the weekends, just to spend the day. He would whine, and cry, and he'd fuss and say how much he loved me, how much he wanted me back. How all this is gonna be different. He's gonna build a room down in the cellar for the kids, you know, and on, and on, and on. He's gonna buy me a car, which he promised me when I left the shelter. All these things he's gonna do for me.

And then I started thinking, well, after all this he's been telling me, I'm not gonna get that out of any other man, any strange man, you know. That's what kind of made me think if he *is* sincere, it would be worth it going back. But I can't be sure he's sincere. He'd promise me the world, and then get me back there and there'd be no world left.

Then I thought . . . he's always preaching to me too. How I sinned, how I've done this and this is bad and that's bad . . . you know. He says, "You've really sinned; you have to ask for God's forgiveness."

And I asked him, I said, "If I came back would I be . . . have to do . . . would everything be fifty-fifty?" As far as doing what I want to do, when I want, and whatever—have my own freedoms?" "Well," he says, "You're supposed to be submissive to your husband." So I said okay, that's all I wanted to hear. That's just what he wants.

I want to be my own boss. If I fall on my face, I fall on my face. I was kind of teetering on whether to go back because I'm afraid of being alone, afraid of raising the kids by myself. I was really scared. I thought maybe it would be better *to* go back . . . but I kind of like being alone. Because, you know, I can go out of the house and I don't have to tell anybody where I'm going. And I don't have to worry about coming back if I don't want to come back.

So you like being on your own?

I know one thing. I'm not even divorced yet and I've got the name "divorced person." "Divorced woman." From my family, you know. "Keep your husbands away from her." That's another reason. They're all giving me this flack about being divorced, without a man, this type of thing. Watch out for your husbands and all this. They're already starting this, and they're not joking.

It's such a hassle and it's part of why I was thinking last week of just going home. Another thing that really brought me down low was I went to the furniture store and applied for credit so I could get a living room set and a washing machine. One hundred dollars for a washing machine, right? And the store said, no, you haven't been working long enough. It really bothers me. This winter I can't walk to the laundromat, and it's going to be hard getting to the grocery store too. I figured if I could establish credit at the furniture store, then maybe I could get credit for a car.

When I discovered all these things not happening, the nearest thing I could think of was, you know, run. Run back. I even had dreams of . . . running. All night long. It's almost like I was running around the streets. I had gone to bed that night thinking I can't take this. I have to think about it and make a decision. I went to bed, and I cried myself to sleep, prayed all night, cried all night. I finally said, "That's enough." I can't take no more. So I went to sleep. And I dreamed about running, which is just what I would be doing—running back to him because I couldn't take the pressure outside. That's when I decided I can't do that; I've got to stop running. If I fall on my face, I fall on my face. If I live without a living room set for the rest of my life, at least I'll do it by myself. I'm not depending on him for anything.

Another thing. He went out and bought the kids shoes, which he hasn't done for months. Oh, he's getting more generous. Every little thing was working on me to go back, to go back, to go back. All the things were falling apart, plus Denise was sick . . . this all happened the same week and I was about ready to scream.

It is very difficult, I know. In any separation or divorce, there is a lot of ambivalence.

Yeah. But I think—a lot of the reason I made the decision to stay was because I'd be giving up an apartment, a job, a chance to go to school. Why give up everything? Give up school and the chance to get paid for it while I'm doing it? I couldn't do that being back with Ed. He said he'd get a loan out to send me to school. Big deal. I don't want him to send me to school. I want to do it on my own.

Of course, I haven't told him this yet. I talk brave when I'm not around him, but when I'm around him, it's just like I'm a mouse again. I fall right back into the old pattern of "Yes, sir"—that type of thing. Don't do anything to get him angry . . . don't stand up to him or he'll get angry.

When he came here this weekend, I wasn't expecting him. I was going along doing my own thing, the kids were out playing. All of a sudden he appears. And he runs over and kisses me and hugs me, and I want to say "Bluuuugh." Yet I don't fight it! I go along with it so there won't be any hassle. Even though I don't want him pawing me and hanging all over me, I just go along with it and let it happen.

It all boils down to if I'm not going to be nice to him, he's not going to be nice. Or he's going to be nasty. If he was so super-religious as he says he is, he wouldn't be throwing these threats around. He wouldn't be saying, "If you don't mind me, you're gonna be punished." He's got to know that I ain't gonna mind him.

It's strange. I feel so secure and so brave when he's not around, but the minute he comes back around again, you know. . . . With him out of the way I was all right, but the minute he started coming and staying, even though I wasn't having sex with him, it was still that he was all over me all the time. I didn't have to do it but he was still all over me, pawing me. It was almost like I wanted to say go ahead and get it over with and leave me alone. Just like before. If I'd say no, he'd just paw me. And still . . . he hasn't given up any of those feelings or attitudes as far as sex is concerned. To him, it's his privilege. When he wants it, as he said, I'm supposed to be submissive.

Does he see the kids?

The kids enjoy seeing him. He does spend more time with me than he does with them, though, and I have to speak to him about it. His main reason to be up here is to see the kids. He always says, "Go out and play," and takes me in the bedroom. And he says we'll talk for a while. We end up talking for four to five hours, and the kids are still playing. I tell him that the reason he's here is to visit with his children, and he says, "Oh, I visited with them." So it isn't really a concern . . . he just wants to straighten out our relationship. He doesn't want . . . the kids are his way, really.

I'm hoping that I can get a restraint on him about visitation for when I'm not around. So he won't take them. I'm worried that he might take them. He says he never would because he'd ruin the kids. I said that's right—they would end up hating him. But he's threatened it so many times that it's always in the back of my head.

I'm definitely going through with the divorce. Just this last week I've had doubts, but I'm doing it.

How do you feel about other men now?

I don't want a new relationship right away. I hope eventually I find another man. But I'm going to be very careful. I would like to go out, have a good time, meet . . . a lot of people. I don't want to fall right into another relationship. I don't want to be . . . I've always been attracted to the men that take over, you know. Do things for me and run my life—the whole bit. I don't want to do that any more. I'd like to have a lot of friends, just people to talk to besides the kids. I spend all my time with the kids.

I'm lonely—very lonely. And I think that's why it looked so good, going back home. And I wouldn't be alone. But once I thought about last winter, and how trapped I was, how isolated and caged and . . . no way would I ever go back there. I took an awful lot of drugs to get out of that cage and I never did. I never got out of it until I stopped the drugs. And stopped staying with him. And now the door is open a little bit. Not completely, because I don't feel I'm a total person yet. But it's open a little bit. And I can almost see the light at the end of the tunnel.

CHAPTER 7

A General Systems Model of Wife Battering

Family violence is an area of research that lends itself well to a general systems approach. This approach provides the tools to analyze the social processes that lead to violence. Many of the questions policy makers, researchers, and victims want to answer focus on the processes. For example: How does violence become an established pattern over time? How can that pattern, which often involves escalation, be changed?

Despite many references to the need for a more comprehensive and dynamic framework for studying families (Broderick, 1971; Hoffman, 1971; Hill, 1971; Speer, 1970), there are very few examples applying a systems approach to the family (Straus, 1973; Kantor & Lehr, 1975; Raush *et al.*, 1974). As Broderick and Smith (1979) point out, we often do not ask systems questions. In addition they point out that investigation of change over time is seldom attempted, because it requires before and after studies.

The purpose of this chapter is to use the conceptual tools of systems theory to present a model of changing phenomena over time in wife-battering relationships. First, a temporal/logical model of the wife-battering process is presented in six stages. At each stage attention is directed to how different levels of feedback control affect the ongoing processes within the system. In the latter half of this chapter the history of wife-battering processes is presented in a flow chart. This chart includes visual presentation of the strata and temporal/logical hierarchies discussed by Broderick and Smith (1979).

General systems theory is treated here as an approach to aid understanding. This is primarily a descriptive study not a testing of theoretical propositions. Throughout this section comparisons with research using other theoretical tools will provide a guide to assessing the strengths and weaknesses of the systems approach.

THE SIX-STAGE MODEL OF WIFE BATTERING

The stages in this model tend to form a temporal/logical hierarchy, although they are not arranged so that one must necessarily precede or follow another. In some cases, they represent somewhat arbitrary punctuation of a process of adaptive change over the life history of a system.

Stage 1. The Establishment of the Family System

In this initial stage of any family system, the groundwork is laid for ongoing patterns of interaction, boundaries are established, and rules evolve which govern the system. In the case of family systems that include violence, it is important to know how the family system was established to allow patterns of violence to develop.

Three systems questions must be addressed at this stage:

1. How did patterns established in other systems affect the new family system?

2. How did the commitment that established the family boundaries evolve?

3. What rules concerning power relationships and the use of violence were part of the family system in this initial stage?

These questions help organize the discussion of how the new family system became established. They also suggest areas that are theoretically important to the long-term goal of a systems theory of family violence.

The first question asks how learned patterns of interaction affect the establishment of the new system. Using the simplest level in the hierarchy of feedback control presented by Broderick and Smith (1979), we can look at the output from other systems that become input for the new system.

At the beginning of any couple relationship, each person has already acquired many historically determined characteristics and behavioral predispositions. They have learned norms, values, and responses relating to conflict processes. A person's history of conflict and violent experiences affects the patterns of conflict and violence in subsequent relationships.

Figure 7-1 presents an illustration of two individuals, represented by A and B, who come together in a relationship which is represented by C. Each of the five factors listed within the circles labeled A and B

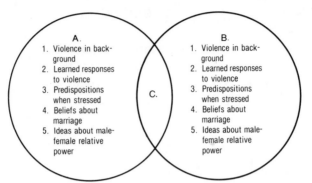

FIG. 7-1. Learned norms, values, and responses of individuals relating to conflict processes within marriage or a couple relationship.

can affect the processes of conflict that become part of the relationship C.

A relatively high percentage of both the men and the women in this sample had experienced violence in their backgrounds (see Table 3-2). Straus *et al.* (1980) found that if a person was physically beaten by parents, or observed violence between parents, then as an adult he/she was many times more likely to be physically violent to a child and/or to a spouse.

If violence has been acceptable in other systems, people are likely to respond the same way to violence in new systems. The monitoring function of cybernetic control is not as likely to signal negative feedback as it is if there had not been violence in other systems.

In addition to the active role, the responses to violence as a child may become patterned and affect responses to violence in later relationships. For example, Elizabeth and Paula had both developed a passive and disassociative response to violence as children, and later maintained the same pattern of response to the violence of their husbands.

Just as responses to violence become patterned, dealing with stress also can be patterned. These patterns, learned early, can affect how one deals with stress within marriage. Megargee (1972) and Geen (1972) discuss how the frustration–aggression link is mediated by social learning. Inhibitions to aggression can be learned as can the aggressive response when frustration is present; therefore, the histories of each of the individuals that make up the relationships contain a schedule of social learning that may affect the way in which people later deal with stress.

Since family relationships are inherently stressful (Gelles & Straus, 1979) and characterized by conflict (Sprey, 1969, 1971), the learned responses to stress and frustration are important.

At this stage in a couple relationship, a boundary has not been established. Feedback tends to be governed in this case by the other systems each person is a part of. For these couples, the important other systems included their family of origin, sometimes another marriage or relationship, and work and friendship systems. Each member of the new couple had learned patterns of behavior in those other systems, and their initial responses to meeting a new person reflect those learned patterns.

Why did women increase their commitment to the men even when in some cases there was evidence about possible violence?

If you recall Paula's life history, Ed had been very rough with her before they were married, and she did later marry him and lived with him for 10 years.

To understand Paula and many other women like her, it is important to examine the second major question in this section: *How did the commitment evolve over time that established the boundaries of the system?*

When the women reported a history of violence in the man's past, many spontaneously said they had not know about the violence when they first got involved. Many of the women currently feel there may be a relationship between the violence in the man's early life and the present patterns of violence, but they report that at the time they were getting involved they did not consider it something to be worried about. Generally women were sympathetic, rather than wary, in response to revelations of this kind. For example:

He got picked on. His mother picked him up by the ears and he told me he had broomsticks broken over his back and everything.

This response also applies to revelations of violence in a man's previous marriage or relationship. The women in these cases did not consider, at first, that prior violent behavior might have any influence on their relationships. At first the women accepted the man's explanation—for example, "She always was nagging me."

This pattern of dismissal or sympathy means the women did not focus on past violence as a warning signal for future violence. The overlooking of possible warning signals even extended to the case where the man had hit them before they married or started living together. In 13% of the cases, the first incident of violence preceded marriage or living together. In an additional 10% of the cases, the women were living with the men when the first incident happened, yet they later married the men. One woman said,

It took me two or three weeks to believe it, but during that time he was fine. He was just like nothing had ever happened the next day. A few weeks later I asked him why he got so upset. He said something else had happened

In this case the incident appeared to the woman to be totally out of character. She had another ongoing interaction that was encouraging her to make a commitment to the man. Her reactions of fear and disbelief received negative feedback because of the return to normal activity. Thus the response of disbelief and shock tended to diminish, and other factors influencing her to make a commitment became dominant.

Sprey (1969) discussed how marriage in American society may be the result of coercive influences of the social structure. Social expectations, emotional, legal, and material rewards, and the lack of acceptable alternative roles, especially for women, tend to make marriage an almost universal commitment. This coercive influence may outweigh the impact of incidents of violence that occur prior to the marriage or living-together commitment.

Positive feedback responses from friends, parents, relatives, and others in the social environment encourage commitment. This is generally true, but it may be particularly true for the woman who is pregnant by the man, has a child by the man, or is divorced and has children. The role of single parent or divorced woman is heavily stigmatized in American society. Positive feedback from others encourages women in these situations to make a choice of commitment. This may result in women committing themselves to relationships that they suspect may have problems later. In one case, a woman was about to get married and had invited her mother to meet the man. As she says,

Mother came up and met Fred. It was not good. They fought and she left. Fred got drunk and had gone to bed and broken a lamp. He accused me of breaking the lamp, then he went at me, threw me down on the bed and started choking me. I tried to rationalize it. He had put

up with a lot from my mother. He had blacked out. It was not really him. It frightened me, but I tried to forget; but it would flash. It made me a little less open until I was able to convince myself that it was all in my head. I kept having these nightmarish daydreams, however. It made it difficult to greet him like nothing was wrong.

The woman's mother in this case did not like the man, but she did not pressure her daughter not to marry him. In America we view marriage as the goal and most valued state for adults. In addition, women are taught to "get a husband" from the time they are little, rather than to think about whether they want to get married and carefully evaluate the person they may marry. These larger social system influences have an impact on the patterns of interaction within systems.

From a systems perspective, the increasing commitment represents a positive feedback loop. Once an initial step has been made in the direction of commitment, the rules of the larger social system and the internal rules of each member of the system determine the feedback loop. In general, society encourages pair bonding and this often leads to an escalation of the original commitment. This is called a positive or deviation-amplifying feedback loop.

The oppositive effect would occur when the rules of the larger social system tend to dampen any new variation in the system. In the example mentioned above, the woman involved or her mother could have acted in ways to discourage any further increase in the commitment. They did not, however. If their own rules for appropriate behavior had excluded violence completely, the cybernetic monitor would have led to a negative or deviation dampening feedback loop.

Once a commitment has been made, the next question is: *What rules concerning the use of violence, and how power will be distributed, have already been established?*

In general, people are ignorant of the actual, as opposed to the expected or mythical, realities of marriage. What the actual expectations of each of the people are for marriage affects the experiences they have after they are married. One particular area of expectations for marriage that may affect conflict processes is the area of ideas about relative male–female power. As reported in Chapter 3, the couples in this sample have higher than normal rates of both male-dominated relationships and female-dominated relationships. It's not possible to know what their expectations were when they first got married, but the skewed relationships may have been the result of ideas about the relative male–female power relationship that they brought into the relationship from other systems.

These issues that can affect conflict processes within marriage are significant in any relationship. They may be particularly significant in these violent couples. The women often knew little about the men when they made a commitment to them. For example, Paula said,

We did not know anything about each other. The first three months of marriage—or the first six months, 'cause we were living together three months—we spent in bed. That's all he wanted to do. We didn't have time to do nothing.

In general, cybernetic feedback processes work to maintain the system once it is established. There were signs of these processes even at the early stages. In two of the cases in which violence preceded the marriage or living together commitment, the man's behavior was a response to the woman's attempts to break off the relationship. The following quotation illustrates what happened.

I broke off with him. I didn't want to see him. He came and he threw snowballs at the windows of the room where my sister's baby was sleeping. I was afraid he would hurt the baby. I called the police and he was taken. After he was released, he came to the hospital where I was working. He cornered me, and put a knife to my throat and threatened me. He was mad because of what the police had done to him.

The woman went back with this man right after the incident. Later she married him. To understand why she did so, we must understand her perspective. I asked her who she thought was responsible for this incident. She said, "Maybe I was, because I didn't want to go with him, but he was responsible for his own actions." She is confused, but she did associate some aspects of her own behavior with the violence. She reasoned that if she did not leave again, then the violence would stop. In effect, her compliance was positive feedback to the violence. The compliance satisfied his goals, and enhanced the likelihood of his using violence again under similar circumstances.

These new family systems were established in ways that allowed violent patterns to develop. Histories of violence in other systems of either the man, the woman, or both, determined responses to violence in the new system. In addition, beliefs about marriage and the male–

female power dimension determined the most likely patterns in the new system.

There were warning signals of future violence in many cases, and this included men who coerced the women to have a relationship with them even when the women wanted to separate. The most striking aspect of this stage is the presence of and/or potential for both conflict and violence.

Stage 2. The First Incident of Violence

The beginning of the relationship and the first incident of violence overlap in some cases, as suggested by previous discussion. When the first incident of violence occurred, 13% of the women were neither married to, nor living with, the man; 35% were living together, 48% were married, and 3% were separated.

The following systems question focuses the discussion of the first incident of violence: *How did the sequence of interaction between the couple at the time of the first incident affect the possibility of future incidents?* A systems approach directs attention to the mechanisms of feedback control to answer this question. The cybernetic functions within each person's internal system and within the family system determine feedback to violence.

First, the internal system of each member monitors input in comparison with its expressive and/or instrumental goals (see Gelles & Straus, 1979, for a discussion of expressive and instrumental goals of violent behavior). If the violent person's goals are satisfied, positive feedback to the new behavior occurs.

In addition to the internal goals of each person, system maintenance goals also act as monitors in the cybernetic process. The case of coercive violence following a woman's attempts to leave the relationship (discussed in Stage 1) illustrates how violence is used to achieve system maintenance goals.

The victim's internal system also monitors the evidence as new input. Although all but one of the women reported that the incident had a strong impact on them at the time, they overwhelmingly reported (28 out of 31 cases) that they thought it was an isolated incident that probably would not happen again. Two of the three who did express doubt about it happening again were women who had experienced violence before, one from parents and one from a previous partner. Almost all of the women (93%) were willing after that first incident to forgive and forget—or at least to forgive. This response, although admirable in some respects, represents positive feedback similar to the feedback message of compliance.

A high percentage (86%) of the women reported that they *felt* angry at their men at the time of the first incident, but they did not respond in angry, retaliatory, or rejecting ways. Well over half (64%) sought no intervention after the incident and did not leave the house. Each of these responses would represent negative feedback to new input. This pattern of seeking little, if any, help or social control after the first incident of violence represents positive feedback to the new behavior, violence, which encourages the likelihood of more violence in a deviation-amplifying loop.

Why didn't the new input elicit angry, retaliatory, or rejecting responses? Most people would be outraged if assaulted by a stranger. Within a family system, social norms and family norms emphasize the maintenance of the system often at the cost of pain and suffering. For example, marriage vows often include, "for better or worse." In addition, the patriarchal structure of society partially legitimizes the use of physical coercion by the man on his wife. The norms, values, and legitimate authorization of violence within the social system for use against a wife make violence part of the standards of acceptable input into the system for some people. Surprisingly, some women do resist violence from their men and seek help or social control. Seeking help is a stronger norm violation than the actual incident of violence.

The structural legitimization of a man hitting his wife leads to her lack of response when violence first happens. This is consistent with Straus's proposition (1973) that "most violence is either denied or not labeled as deviance."

The return to normal activity after the first incident of violence also represents positive feedback to the violence. Given the positive feedback, violence is encouraged. There is a greater likelihood it will happen again.

Systems models emphasize the branching function. After violence first occurs, the theoretical alternatives are that it will never occur again, or that it will recur with a wide range of patterns of escalation. The women in this sample had all been hit more than once, but the patterns of violence ranged from two incidents to almost daily life-threatening violence. Unfortunately, this study does not provide a basis for understanding those couples in which there is only one incident of violence. It does, however, provide a unique data base to explore how patterns become stabilized over time.

Stage 3. Stabilization of the Violence

Systems theory predicts that behavior which receives positive feedback will increase. If a deviation-amplifying loop occurs, violence is likely to become an established part of the ongoing interaction patterns within the system. As we saw earlier, the first acts of violence often received positive feedback, making it likely they would happen again. If violence involves an unacceptable pattern of input for either member of the system, an important system question arises: *How does the cybernetic function within the total system operate to allow violence to escalate? To the extent that there is conflict between the internal goals of two members of the system, how does the interactional system between them evolve?*

Comparison of male and female violent behavior in this study indicates that even though some of the women were violent, they were more likely than the men to be victimized and injured. Being victimized and injured was not an acceptable outcome for any women in this study. In other words, none were masochistic. The escalation continued in most cases, however, despite the cybernetic function of their own internal system.

To understand escalation a systems theory approach suggests exploration of (1) the sequence of events, (2) the alternatives to the escalation possible within the system, and (3) the possibilities for morphogenesis through corrective responses.

First, in the sequence of events, one act of violence brings about change in the system which intensifies the conflict itself, and further increases the likelihood of violence. This process has been referred to within systems theory as a "runaway" (Haley, 1963). Each act of violence is grounds for anger and further conflict. An example of a "runaway" is feuding between families. After a while each forgets where it really started, and they become concerned only with getting revenge for the last acts of the other party. Some of the women did fight back; others withdrew emotionally. Each of these responses elicited further violence. The violence in some cases appeared to be related to system maintenance goals and in other cases to the goals of the men to maintain dominance.

Many of the woman did not fight back. However, they tended to give in to the man to stop the violence. For example, one woman said,

As long as I went along with him it was all right. His mother made us go to his sister's for Thanksgiving. I objected. He knocked me around and put his fist through the wall. I went so he wouldn't hit me any more.

The woman's objections were an unacceptable alternative. His continued violence represented negative feedback. Consequently, she was less likely to object in the future. He achieved his objective goals by the use of violence. He also established the dominance within the system of his own goals. At this point the rules of the family system were that he had the dominant position.

When she gave in, she complied with those rules and her response represented positive feedback to the violence. The violence soon became an established pattern.

Once escalation has occurred, corrective action within the system often does not work. When it became clear to the battered women that no response they used would stop the violence, they tried different ways to correct the behavior. They talked to police, family, and friends.

But escalation also leads to polarization. Relatives and friends of bickering couples take sides in the argument. Scherer *et al.* (1975) illustrate the sociometry of polarization. In their model the two separate nexuses of polarization appear to have equal numbers of alliances. In reality, when a man and woman are in a battering relationship, the polarization that leads to others taking sides is affected by conditions in the social structure. Dobash and Dobash (1978) documented the reactions of police, medical personnel, and legal professionals to women when they sought help. Dobash and Dobash also discuss how family and friends reacted when a woman sought help. The title of their article well illustrates the thesis of the paper: "With Friends like These Who Needs Enemies: Institutional Supports for the Patriarchy and Violence against Women." Women's complaints were often not answered, and not taken seriously. Paula's experience illustrates what could happen when the police actually did come:

I kicked him out and I called the cops. They came in and walked around the house and said, "Well, he's not here." I said, "No, of course not. He ran away when he heard me calling the cops." They looked around and saw all his Marine Corps things on the walls and they said,

"Well, if he's a Marine, he can't be all that bad." And out they walked. They said, "We'll keep an eye out for him and if we see him, we'll grab him." And that was all that was done.

Negative feedback from outsiders to new behavior such as seeking help dampens the chance of it becoming part of the system. Over time women's attempts to get help from formal social control agencies increased only slightly (23% for the first incident, 20% for the most significant incident, and 35% for the last incident). Change within the system, after escalation has occurred, depends on finding alternative responses.

Extreme isolation is both a result of being unable to find alternatives and a further step in the stabilization of the pattern. The stigma associated with family problems in general and family violence in particular led women to hide the situation from others. The boundaries of the family's system became relatively closed. As Paula said, "I would never tell anybody that he was hitting me." Paula's words echoed again and again in accounts by the other women. As the violence became Paula's dominant concern, she became more isolated and could not involve herself in other things. She said,

I'd keep low. I didn't want to do anything and I didn't want to go anywhere. I didn't want to visit anybody.

Whereas the women's feelings and attempts to get help were often neglected and criticized, the men seemed to have an alliance with police and others—an implicit alliance. This was illustrated by Debbie when she described how the police came into the yard, talked with her husband, and left. The nature of the implicit alliance was clear when Bob came in the house and said one of the policemen was his friend. Generally, when the boundaries of the family system were passed to get help from the larger social system, the man's position received positive feedback and the woman's position received negative feedback.

There were periods when the family interaction was consistent with "normal" family patterns. This encouraged women to think change was possible within the system. Most of the women wanted their relationships to last. Their goals included maintaining the family system. One woman said, "Everything I have is invested in that marriage." Even when the women came to the shelter, 23% said they wanted to go back to the relationship if new terms could be worked out. We know from learning theory that an intermittently reinforced schedule is the hardest to extinguish. The man's "normal" periods or his contrite periods (Walker, 1979) encouraged the women to stay in the system even after the pattern of violence had become well stabilized.

When the corrective responses of cybernetic feedback do not keep interaction among the members of the system within acceptable ranges, a shift may occur to a different level of feedback control called morphogenesis or metachange. Morphogenesis involves a change in the basic rules of transformation within the system. For example, if women are unable to contain the violence within "acceptable" limits, they may change their internal goals. They may decide to talk to other people or seek outside help, both of which represent crossing the boundaries of the system. If they receive positive feedback, this enhances the possibility of either minor corrective action within the system or more fundamental change. If they are not able to correct the system, the pattern of violence will be further strengthened.

Stage 4. The Choice Point

When ongoing patterns are no longer tolerated, there is a possibility for more fundamental change. A systems approach suggests we must explore the following questions to understand the possibilities for fundamental change:

1. When do patterns of wife battering become intolerable?
2. Are there criteria for intolerability other than amount of violence?

When I began this research, I expected that the most recent incident would have been the most violent and would have precipitated the move. Generally that was not the case. The incident that stood out in the women's minds as most important and most critical in their decisions to move occurred a few weeks to several months prior to their coming to the shelter. In one case, the most critical incident occurred eight years prior to arrival at the shelter.

Scherer *et al.* (1975, p. 273) state, "There appears to be in many conflicts a special period (which may be quite brief in terms of time) when a turn is reached. It is distinguished by a new, intense and different level of interaction." In their model they call this stage "Crisis," but they admit the term is ambiguous and that they cannot do much to clarify it. The information given by the women in this sample may help clarify this concept of crisis in conflict processes over time, particularly information about the incident which stood out in the minds of the women as being most important. How does a system characterized by stabilized patterns of violence reach a crisis point? Systems theory suggests that for change to occur, new input has to be processed by the system. When women described the most critical incident, three different themes were reported by a significant number of women. These three illustrate the kinds of new input that mark a choice point:

   1. Fear the children would be hurt.
   2. Resentment at the husband for letting the children see their mother beaten.
   3. The exposure of the violent pattern to people outside the family.

The first theme, fear the children would be hurt, was a critical new input Elizabeth talked about as the critical point. For Debbie, it was when Bob took her out in the woods and told their son she was a "lying bitch," then assaulted her in front of him. Another of the 31 women described this scene:

Brian [their son] had come home from college, and he wanted money. He [the husband] wanted me to go borrow money at the bank. I said, "Go get it yourself." Brian said, "You two are always fighting about money. I'm sick of it." He [the husband] got Brian down on the floor. I said, "Leave him alone." That's when he came at me, pounded me, and threw me down on the bed. He ripped all my clothes. I was so badly bruised and bloody that my two daughters had to carry me into the bedroom and wash me off. One of the girls went to the neighbors and told her, "He is killing my mother." She came over and said, "You leave her alone." He whipped around and put his fist through the double doors. He told her, "This is my house."
   I was ashamed to have my girl friend see me in that condition. I think he would have killed me if she hadn't come in. I was also ashamed that my children had to see my body unclothed.

The woman who told this story never forgave him for that incident. She could not forget the shame she had experienced. This was a critical psychological point for her, but she did not move. As she said, "I went to the bank, I'll tell ya." The system was still intact at this point, but new input had become a part of the pattern of violence. In addition the incident altered the boundaries that had formerly been drawn around the violence.

From a systems theory perspective, if the family is relatively closed to outside input, the impact of norms and constraints in the larger social system is less. As the violence becomes stabilized, it also becomes reified. Once established a pattern takes on legitimacy, because it is what has existed. Many of the women seemed to have lost contact with the social evaluation of the extreme acts of violence. As outsiders became aware of the violent incidents, the boundaries of the closed system budged and this further enhanced the chances for change. A process of reevaluation began at this point, but the women did not move immediately.

A systems approach suggests that the critical incident is a decision point from which the pattern of interaction within the system branches in different directions. The new input may produce system morphogenesis leading to new patterns of acceptable reponses. The violence may also escalate still further, or the system may go through the level of feedback control described by Broderick and Smith (1979) as "Reorientation or Conversion."

The women in this study had all sought help at a shelter for battered women, so this data base cannot provide insight into other directions the system interaction may take after the choice point. This study does, however, provide an opportunity to explore a very important path some women take after that critical incident.

Stage 5. Leaving the System

At earlier stages in the wife-battering process, all input was monitored in reference to system maintenance goals. At earlier stages attempts were made to restructure the pattern of violence to maintain the family as a system. In this stage there is a process taking place that may lead to a fundamental reorientation.

A systems approach suggests the following questions may be important to understanding if and how reorientation occurs:

1. How do the boundaries of the system shift?
2. How does one member of the system leave to possibly become a member of another system?
3. How does the battering member of the system respond to attempts by the victim to alter the boundaries of the system?

The time lag reported between the most critical incident and coming to the shelter indicates that for most of the women leaving was a process that occurred gradually over time.

At the choice point, the women made a psychological move in the direction of leaving the system, but what made them leave when they actually did? A systems approach suggests exploring first if they have alternative sources of feedback outside the boundaries of the original system.

The fact that a large percentage of the women had been close to another person for at least a few months indicates women in those cases sought and found alternate sources of feedback outside the system in the period between the critical incident and the time they came to the shelter. Many of the women spontaneously mentioned that the other person also had been beaten or that the person helped them by talking about the beatings. The presence of a confidante was found by Lowenthal and Haven (1968) to significantly help people going through psychological and physical stress. The confidantes and the battered women in this study formed a bridging relationship that spanned the boundaries of the original system.

This bridging relationship was important, because the family system that had been their total involvement for so long required a new system—a supportive system to act in the bridging role between the original family system and the larger social system. As Paula said,

She [a confidante] had been an abused wife, and I talked to her a lot because we could communicate with the things that had happened to her. She is the one that really helped me a lot—being able to talk to somebody that it had happened to, too. And she would always say, "I don't know why you stay." I didn't, you know, but I didn't have any way out. At least I thought I didn't.

This excerpt illustrates that staying with or leaving the abusive man is not a calculated, rational decision women make at a particular point. Leaving is a process that occurs over time. With Ed, Paula responded according to patterns that had gradually become stabilized within the system.

As the boundaries of the system opened, women became more aware of new opportunities available in other systems. Public educational programs and media coverage reached some women at this point. Paula said,

I use the name "battered wife" because that's what they use on TV. "Battered wives." In fact, when I saw it, I had told Ed, "Come in and watch this with me. That's you and me on TV there." He just laughed about it. He thought it was funny. But it was true, you know.

Publicity about family violence may lead women to seek protection against victimization. The opportunity for help also has to be there, however. Most of the women had made attempts to leave before the time they came to the shelter. Some went to family; some stayed out in the woods or on the street all night, as Elizabeth did; some went to friends as Debbie did; others went elsewhere. These arrangements tended to be unsatisfactory. Friends and family could not provide the housing and support for the women and their children. Other battered women who have had the same experiences provided the best source of support.

Family—and professionals, in some cases—turned women away when they asked for help. A family doctor responded to a woman he had just patched up in this way:

You took a vow when you got married to love and to cherish for better or worse 'till death do you part. Now go home with him. You are never going to change him. This is the way he shows his love.

Later the same woman was hospitalized with serious back injuries. Another doctor told her at that time her body would not take any more abuse. The next time she would be dead. For the first time in 28 years, somebody had supported her leaving. She came to the shelter directly from the hospital. Her injuries from years of abuse are so extensive, however, she will never again be completely healthy.

Women go through a gradual process of leaving the family system. The process involves first a bridging of the boundaries of the system. New responses on the part of the woman to the victimizing behavior included seeking help from family, friends, and social control agents. The new responses represent input into both the original system and into other systems that are becoming established outside the original system. The feedback to the new responses is critical. Within the original system, attempts to get help or leave at this stage elicited strong negative feedback from the men whose goals of maintaining the system had been challenged.

Within other newly forming systems such as friendship systems, the women's expression of their frustrations and expressions of wanting to leave tended to receive positive feedback leading in some cases to a deviation-amplifying loop.

At this stage, there is conflict between the original family system, and new emerging systems. The outcome depends on the strength of different goals within the two systems and within the individual woman. Does the woman want to maintain the original system? If she does, the feedback from other systems will not be as important as the feedback from within the original system. If she does want to leave, however, the feedback from new emerging systems will be more important. Shifts occur over time in the importance of the two systems. Without a new system to become involved in and without strong positive feedback within the system, reorientation and conversion are unlikely to occur.

Stage 6. Resolution or More of the Same?

A systems approach emphasizes branching and the possibilities of multiple outcomes. A major decision point often follows the stage of reorientation and conversion. New input has been processed by the system, and some basic structural changes may be occurring. Resolution, however, requires stabilizing new structural patterns.

This approach raises three central questions related to how systems processes affect wife battering after a woman's stay at a shelter:

1. After the stay at the shelter, will the original family system be restructured in a way that the cybernetic processes will dampen the likelihood of future violence?

2. If women choose not to return to the men after the shelter, are they successful in establishing new and satisfying systems to replace the original family system?

3. How likely is it that women who do return to the original system will return to the same patterns of interaction including violent behavior?

Twenty-four of the 31 women in the original sample were reinterviewed six months after they came to the shelter. Of those reinterviewed, 58% had returned to the man, at least temporarily, after leaving the shelter. Sixteen percent had reconciled and later left. Forty-two percent were married to and/or living with the man at the time of the second interview.

Of all the follow-up couples, 54% reported at least one incident of violence in that interim period. Of those who returned to the man 75% reported violence. Of those who returned and later left, 50% reported at least one violent incident. Those who returned and did not later leave reported a 62% violence rate. The women in the last category—those who returned and never left—reported the highest percent of violent incidents. Returning to a relationship that has an established pattern of violence is in some cases similar to compliance to the man's demands at earlier stages. If the system has not been restructured, the return indicates the acceptance of established patterns. This represents positive feedback which enhances the likelihood of future violence.

In most cases the amount and seriousness of violence in the six months after the shelter decreased. A high percentage of the women who returned to the man, however, reported at least one incident of violence. At this point there is a possibility the pattern of violence may escalate again through the same set of stages. Often women return to the shelters. Six of the women in the original sample did in fact return to the shelter during the six months between the two interviews.

There are two other options in addition to returning to an earlier stage of conflict. The first is to never return to the original family system; the second is to return, but with some restructuring of the patterns in the system. As Scherer et al. (1975) suggested, basic restructuring is probably rare.

Of those who never returned to the man after they left the shelter, 44% reported at least one violent incident with the man. So, even if the woman does not return, there is no assurance that she will not be involved in violent incidents. In those violent incidents the man attempted to coerce the woman to return to the original family system. In some cases the coercive attempts worked. Debbie returned to Bob under those conditions.

Other women resisted coercion but suffered the consequences. For example, one man broke into two different apartments the woman moved to, and once raped her. Physical distance, separate residences, and legal restraining orders did little to prevent violence. The man had been under a restraining order when the rape incident occurred. Authorities would not pursue the rape charge on the grounds the woman previously had lived with the man. When he appeared in court, his case was continued for several months and he was told to stay away from the woman. The legal system does not provide adequate protection for women under these circumstances. The boundaries of the original family system continue to exist in the view of others in the larger social structure.

The second option—of returning home with some change—is possible. On the basis of an informal assessment, 8 of the 14 women who did return to the man were in systems that had been restructured six months after the stay at the shelter. Examples of restructuring included: the man and the woman going to counseling together; the man and/or woman getting help for alcoholism; or the woman developing some outside interests. Each of these represents a new alternative to the established pattern. Of the 8 cases, however, 4 later left the man. That left 4 cases in which I thought there had been some fundamental change in the patterns of interaction between the couples.

Theoretically the shelter provided opportunity for restructuring the system. Some women used the shelter time to negotiate with the man for change in the basic pattern. The shelter offered the women a place to go and safety during this negotiation process. This tended to equalize the power relationship between the man and the woman. Women have traditionally been unable to do this because they had no place to go and were, therefore, in a poor position to negotiate.

Women who chose separation and did not return to the man found restructuring new systems difficult. For example, Paula experienced criticism, prejudice, and little social support for a new life-style alone with her children. Each of these experiences inhibits the fundamental change necessary for complete reorientation and resolution. As Paula's case illustrated, women were often vulnerable at this stage to promises of change from their husbands.

Complete reorientation and resolution is a long and difficult process. Members of the new system must reorient their goals, reestablish boundaries that exclude a former member, and establish new patterns of interaction to maintain that system and satisfy the goal states of the various members of the system.

FLOW CHART OF STABILITY AND CHANGE

Flow charts are a way of summarizing a theory of process over time, such as that presented in the six-stage model. A flow chart captures the "wholeness" of the system and the complexity of the processes that lead to stability and change in system patterns.

Figure 7-2 specifies the processes that move the system, over time, through the six stages of wife battering. Each of the symbols numbered 1 through 15 represents steps or processes in the patterns of wife battering.

Symbols 1, 2, and 3 represent the establishment of the new family system. The learned norms, values, and response options that each member in the relationship brings to the new relationship from other systems affect the conflict processes within the marriage or couple relationship. The area in the figure, labeled 3, is purposively small to reflect the finding that the women in this sample seemed to know little about the men when they became involved.

Symbol 4 in Figure 7-2 summarizes the most frequently cited preceding events for three incidents of violence. Change occurred over time in preceding events. Events which threatened the boundaries of the system were frequently cited, and over time "none" became the most frequent category reflecting the stabilization of the violence independent of stressful events.

Symbol 5 indicates possible sources of standards for system rules of transformation concerning violence. The prior history of using violence, observation of violence, and prior responses to violence, affect the subsequent rules that govern cybernetic feedback.

According to a systems approach the most significant determinant of whether violence becomes a stabilized pattern is cybernetic control. Any new input—such as violence—is monitored in terms of goal states, either the actor's goals or the goals of the system to maintain itself (represented in Symbol 7).

If the appropriate goal states are not satisfied by the violent act, this leads to an alternate response to satisfy that goal state (Symbol 8). If the new response is accepted and satisfies the goal (Symbol 9), the alternative may lead to permanent change in the system. In this case the new response is likely to become a variation in the pattern of ongoing behavior (Symbol 10). If, however, the new response (Symbol 8) does not lead to attainment of goals and/or is not accepted by the system, the violent behavior may receive positive feedback. People may return to an earlier pattern of violence if alternatives don't work. This is more likely after violence has become stabilized as a pattern than it is after the first use of violence.

To return to Symbol 7, if the violence does satisfy the actor's goals or the system maintenance goals, the satisfaction itself may be positive feedback to the violence.

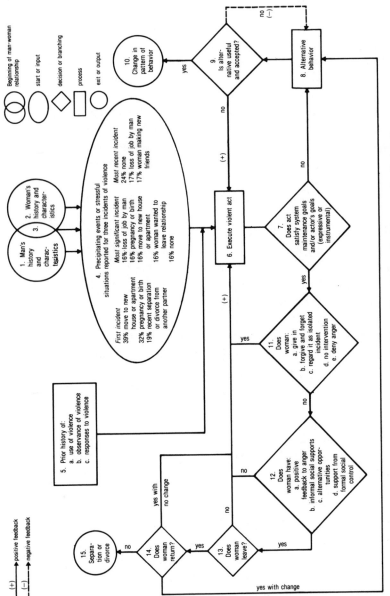

FIG. 7-2. Flow chart of stability and/or change in patterns of wife beating.

Beginning of man-woman relationship

start or input

decision or branching

process

exit or output

(+) → positive feedback
(-) → negative feedback

1. Man's history and characteristics

2. Woman's history and characteristics

3.

4. Precipitating events or stressful situations reported for three incidents of violence

First incident
39% move to new house or apartment
32% pregnancy or birth
19% recent separation or divorce from another partner

Most significant incident
16% loss of job by man
16% pregnancy or birth
16% move to new house or apartment
16% woman wanted to leave relationship
16% none

Most recent incident
24% none
17% loss of job by man
17% woman making new friends

5. Prior history of:
a. use of violence
b. observance of violence
c. responses to violence

6. Execute violent act

7. Does act satisfy system maintenance goals and/or actor's goals (expressive or instrumental)

8. Alternative behavior

9. Is alternative useful and accepted?

10. Change in pattern of behavior

11. Does woman:
a. give in
b. forgive and forget
c. regard it as isolated incident
d. no intervention
e. deny anger

12. Does woman have:
a. positive feedback to anger
b. informal social supports
c. alternative opportunities
d. support from formal social control

13. Does woman leave?

14. Does woman return?

15. Separation or divorce

141

The next step is to look at the women's responses to the violent act. Does the woman: (1) give in? (2) forgive and forget? (3) regard the violent act as an isolated incident? (4) seek no intervention, and/or deny her anger (Symbol 11)?

At this point there are three options. The woman may return with no change, which may be the strongest positive feedback to the pattern of violence and lead to a recycling through the same stages. She may return with change, which leads to rerouting through alternative behavior (Symbol 8) and restructuring of the system. This restructuring is rare, but it is possible. The third alternative is for the woman to leave, separate, and/or divorce. This does not mean the woman will not be beaten again, however, but totally resisting coercive attempts can eventually lead to an end to the pattern of violence.

There are several limitations to this schematic illustration of stability and change in patterns of wife battering. Some of the most important limitations are:

1. The empirical basis for this illustration is a clinical sample which, by definition, excludes processes and decisions that occurred in couples who never developed a stabilized pattern of wife battering or who never sought help at a shelter.

2. Transactions with systems outside the family system are included only as they seemed to directly affect a decision (e.g., Symbol 12). The significant impact of the patriarchal structure of society, and the inequality of opportunities for women, is much more pervasive an influence on the wife-battering process than indicated by this illustration which focuses on the processes within the boundaries of the family system.

3. The processes have been simplified into a model to allow for breadth of understanding. To understand the total complexity, requires examining each case individually.

EVALUATION OF A SYSTEMS THEORY APPROACH

A systems analysis of families who are violent requires a method of gathering data on the entire system. Including material from only the woman's perspective cannot provide an accurate representation of the whole family system. Although it was impossible in this research, the ideal methodology would be to observe the whole family system over the time during which there was violence. In addition to the technical problems, ethical questions arise in this situation. If a researcher observed violence, there would be an ethical obligation to intervene. In light of these problems, a choice must be made either to give up the systems theory approach or give up the pure methodological restrictions of the systems theory. I chose to keep the systems theory approach despite the fact that the source of data reflects the operation of the system as experienced by one of its members rather than the operation of the system itself.

The best approach to developing or testing theory is through the use of different methodologies and independent replication (Campbell & Fiske, 1959). This research must be seen as part of a more comprehensive effort that includes many different research designs.

In addition to the difficulties of methodological implementation, there are other questions that concern the application of systems theory to the issue of wife battering. A systems approach to wife battering leads to an explanation of the violence as the result of system processes. This raises two possible problems with this approach. The first is that the structural patterns of the larger social system are not adequately emphasized in systems analysis that focuses on the family system. Social structural conditions such as the status of women in society, the patterns of economic distribution of resources, the acceptance of violence in society, and the norms for the use of violence in the family exist as social environmental conditions for the families in this study. A systems theory approach that focuses primarily on internal family processes does not emphasize the social structural conditions. This approach can, however, illustrate how structural conditions affect patterns of violence within family systems. This focus on family processes complements other research that primarily addresses the larger social structural issues.

The second question raised by the application of systems theory to the issues of wife beating concerns responsibility. An analysis of wife battering that focuses on family processes implies that the system processes are responsible for the violence happening. Does this explanation relieve individuals of their moral responsibility for destructive acts? No. A systems theory explanation is not an unicausal explanation. Individual characteristics represent input into the system. Systems theory explains violence as the product of interdependent causal processes including the preexisting behavior patterns of system members and the system processes that lead to stability or change in patterns of behavior over time. This does not, however, remove any individual from responsibility for his/her own behavior. What it does is to provide new and important insights into how to deal with the problem. For example, this research found that support from those outside the family system was a determinant of change or stability in the patterns of wife beating. A direct implication of this is that outsiders who downplay the man's violence provide positive feedback that may lead to escalation. This suggests that responses of others to violence affect how patterns became stabilized or altered. Positive feedback to the attempt by a woman to get help can encourage her behavior and thus increase the likelihood of change in the pattern of violence. Women approach medical professionals, mental health professionals, friends, and family to get help, and the response they receive affects the pattern of violence within the family.

These examples suggest how systems theory can be used as a device for uncovering important aspects of what goes on in the family system, between family members, and those outside the family.

The stage model presented in this research can facilitate organizing and understanding the reality of the everyday experiences of being a battered wife. It also focuses attention on process over time, as opposed to analyses of cross-sectional differences in groups which focus on one point in time. A systems approach not only aids understanding of how wife battering becomes an established pattern in families, it also leads to direct suggestions for how that pattern may be changed. This is an approach that promises a great deal both in theory and in practice.

The Research
Process

Often the most important section of a research monograph is that which describes the research process. Presenting the methodology provides other researchers with both a guide for future research of this type and a basis for evaluating the research findings.

Reconstructing the research process is particularly critical when the study is primarily exploratory. In exploratory research, the methodological rules are not as well defined and accepted as traditional methodological techniques. The traditional view of methodology for empirical research emphasizes criteria for choosing a sample, developing and implementing a research design, and developing research instruments which allow the researcher to use the most sophisticated statistical techniques possible. The goal of this traditional methodology is generalizability. Using the most appropriate techniques, we can explain relationships in the entire population through research on a well-chosen sample.

In exploratory research, discovery in a small number of cases takes precedence over generalizability. In-depth study of a small number of cases, provides a basis for knowing what can occur under specific circumstances.

Traditional survey techniques, which gather data at one point in time from structured questionnaires, dominated the family violence field in the 1970s. Early in the decade, the questions raised concerned rates of violence and connections between social characteristics and levels of violence. Given these pressing questions and the knowledge desired, the survey methodology was quite appropriate. Using these techniques researchers found correlations between violence and many social characteristics. These included socioeconomic differences, gender differences, intergenerational patterns, stress, and regional difference (Straus et al., 1980).

In addition, the 1970s saw several attempts to develop theoretical explanations for violence. Trying to develop a theory or theories of family violence led to the observation that many questions had not been answered. For example, how do patterns of violence become established and escalate, and how are these patterns maintained or changed? Straus (1973) suggested the relevance of general systems theory for exploring these questions.

Doing research within the systems theory perspective presents special methodological problems, however. Systems questions focus on change over time. Studying change phenomena within systems is seldom attempted because it requires first, that the system as a whole be studied, and second, that the system be studied over time.

The systems theory approach has been neglected by family sociologists partly because of these difficulties. At the present time, the most well-developed methodology for studying family process is a naturalistic approach (see Kantor & Lehr, 1975; Piotrkowski, 1979).

In the area of family violence, the pure naturalistic approach presents both practical and ethical problems. Family privacy makes observing incidents of violence between a man and his wife difficult at best. But, ethical concerns for the couple's welfare also dictate that even if we could observe violence between the couple, observers should intervene to stop the violence. This intervention would, of course, further block data gathering.

Given these conditions, the pure methodological requirements of systems theory must be reevaluated in light of the importance of the research questions. The importance of knowing how patterns of violence develop, become stabilized, and change over time may outweigh the disadvantages of exploratory methodological techniques. Exploratory research techniques cannot provide a data base for testing hypotheses. These techniques do, however, provide a basis for knowing what can happen in a small number of cases under specific circumstances. Information for a small number of cases can in turn suggest theoretical refinements and ideas for future research.

In the study of change phenomena, Broderick and Smith (1979, p. 122) point out that "even post hoc analyses of these phenomena might shed light on the nature of family systems and the circumstances and preconditions that lead to this highest order of change."

A further consideration in the development of methodological techniques to study these questions is the progress that has been made toward a general systems theory of violence. At this time, there have been suggestions of hypotheses and models (Straus, 1973; Gelles & Straus, 1979; Gelles, 1980). Researchers have not attempted, however, to systematically address these questions in empirical research.

Since empirical knowledge about the important systems questions of this study was unavailable, an exploratory study design was chosen. Exploratory research often uses qualitative naturalistic study techniques. For reasons cited earlier, a naturalistic study was ruled out. A completely qualitative study was also ruled out.

My major focus of both substantive and theoretical concern in this research was the process of change. How did people change over time? For this emphasis of the research, qualitative methods were best suited. What was needed was a record of processes of change. That record could then be analyzed for regularities and patterns that emerged across different incidents or across different cases.

Exploring change phenomena, however, also involves studying how much change has occurred and under what specific conditions. To be able to document change that occurred over time within cases, and change that occurred between different cases under different conditions, some quantitative techniques were also necessary.

On the basis of these two substantive and theoretical considerations, both quantitative and qualitative methods of data collection were used in this research.

DATA-GATHERING TECHNIQUES, RESEARCH SETTING, AND PARTICIPANTS

An ideal group of participants for a study of change in wife-battering patterns would include families with at least three different outcomes to violent relationships: (1) families who were able to control violence within acceptable limits, (2) families in which the woman did not seek help at a shelter despite the fact that violence had become unacceptable, and (3) families in which the woman had sought help at a shelter for battered women.

In the present study, the first two outcomes are not represented, although they are both substantively and theoretically meaningful.

The third group is represented by the 31 women in this study who had sought help at a shelter for battered women. For an exploratory study, this group provides unique opportunities. They have both become involved in patterns of violence, and they also tried to change those patterns. Knowing how some women make the move to change the pattern of violence is important to the development of both policy and a systems theory of the wife-battering process.

Having a small number of participants also presents a unique opportunity. This type of study can explore individual cases in depth, which larger-scale surveys cannot do because of practical considerations.

There are, of course, limitations to this type of study. Exploratory research with a small number of participants cannot provide a basis for making generalizations. In the present research no statements are made about a wider population of all battered women, or even all battered women who go to a shelter.

This is a convenience sample, and other methods could have been used to gather participants. This would, however, have been very impractical and possibly dangerous to women who have already been victimized. Women who have been beaten severely are often not willing to talk to researchers when they are still in their homes, because they fear the men will find out.

The shelter to which all of these women had come provided a setting for interviewing which assured them safety and confidentiality. In addition, their recall of recent incidents was assured by the short time period that had elapsed.

The women also trusted the staff which easily generalized to include my work. All women who came to the shelter in the first six months it was open were interviewed for this study with the exception of a few who stayed less than 48 hours, and two who left before a mutually agreeable time could be arranged. The women who left in a short period of time are likely to be different from the ones who were interviewed. They did not become involved in the actual program of shelter, services, and referral.

Staff at the shelter briefly described my research to all women within 24 hours of their arrival. All cooperated, and many remarked that they would do "anything they could to help," so that "some other woman may not have to suffer what I did." This spirit of cooperation extended to the follow-up interviews for most women, but understandably some women were reluctant to consent to an interview six months after their stay.

I conducted all interviews personally. The former director of the shelter, Mary Price, also participated in the taped interviews with Paula and Elizabeth.

THE FIRST INTERVIEWS

The first interviews were divided into two sections. The first section focuses on descriptive questions about the family system, other relevant systems, and the amount and types of violent acts. This section (questions 1–83, Appendix B) included background information, specifics about their home situation, their early childhood, the employment histories of the women and their men, a list of problems the couple experienced, questions about family power, marital satisfaction, presence of confidantes, and duration of relationship with confidantes.

The Conflict Tactics Scales (Straus, 1979a) were included next. This procedure asks respondents to indicate how often in the past year specific tactics to resolve conflict were used. The Conflict Tactics Scales were presented for parent–child interaction (questions 78–80, Appendix B) and for woman–partner interaction (questions 81–83, Appendix B), but only the woman–partner interaction was analyzed for this research. The specific items from the Conflict Tactics Scales that related to violence are:

    K. Threw something at the other one
    L. Pushed, grabbed, or shoved the other one
    M. Slapped or spanked the other one
    N. Kicked, bit, or hit with a fist

O. Hit or tried to hit with something
P. Beat up the other one
Q. Threatened with a knife or gun
R. Used a knife or gun
S. Other (used to record any additional violent acts)

The second part of the first interview focuses on the history of violence in the family system.

A systems theory emphasizes the sequence of events and change in the sequence of events over time. The questions in this section focus on the sequence of important systems input and output for three incidents of violence.

I asked them to think back to the first time there was any hitting, kicking, pushing, throwing, or anything else they considered violent. When they could recall that specific incident, I asked questions to get a complete picture of that episode (questions 88–105, Appendix B). These included: (1) an account of the incident, (2) what, if any, important events immediately preceded the incident, (3) the status of their relationship at that time, (4) questions about guilt, anger, whether they thought at the time that it was an isolated incident that would not happen again, or if it was part of a pattern of violence, and their willingness to forgive and forget, (5) who or what they thought was responsible for the incident, (6) impact of the incident on the woman, the children, and the relationship at that time, and (7) what happened immediately following the incident—that is, if anyone called was asked to help handle the situation, if they or their man left, and when things returned to normal, if they did.

After a woman finished describing the first incident in detail, I asked the same questions for two other incidents of violence—the most recent incident (questions 106–123, Appendix B), and one incident the woman remembered as being particularly important (questions 124–141, Appendix B).

All of these questions focused the interview, but many times additional information was covered in the interviews and I freely made notes of direct quotations.

THE SECOND INTERVIEWS

Six months after the women first came to the shelter, I contacted them and asked if we could arrange a time to get together for a follow-up interview. Most of the women were glad to hear from me and anxious to talk. I learned as I was going along that I had become quite important to many of the women. I attribute most of this to the fact that our talking was for many the first time anybody had taken the time and interest to listen to their complete stories.

Other women posed more of a problem for the follow-up interview. Four had completely disappeared and had left no forwarding address. Two were evasive and elusive, and one was living in such terror that any attempt to meet has, so far, been too risky for her. Of the 24 completed follow-up interviews, several had moved—some out of state. If they could, we did the interview at the shelter.

The structure of the second interview was similarly divided into two parts. The first included questions on their present situation, changes in employment or their economic situation, questions about their children, and the details of what had happened since they left the shelter. At this time I also repeated each of the Conflict Tactics Scales.

The second part of the interview included the same sets of questions as the first interview, and asked about any violent incidents that had occurred in the preceding six months. The questions from the second interview schedule that were not repeated from the first interview are presented in Appendix C.

These follow-up interviews provided data on the status of the women at the six-month follow-up period. Data from these interviews provided a basis for comparing preshelter and postshelter levels of violence. Those who did return to the partner and those who did not return could also be compared. This study is unique in that it includes longitudinal data from follow-up interviews.

THE TAPED INTERVIEWS

The two structured interviews provided post hoc descriptions of the sequence of events around several incidents of violence. They also provided a basis for comparing specific variables at two points in time. The structured interviews did not, however, capture the complexity of the system processes that affected stability and change in patterns of violence within the family system. To get this information, I collected "personal documents." Bogdan and Taylor use the phrase "personal documents" to refer "to an individual's descriptive, first-person account of the whole or a part of his or her life or an individual's reflection on a specific event or topic" (Bogdan & Taylor, 1975, p. 96). During those interviews, which lasted approximately four hours, the women recounted their personal histories and the histories of their family systems. The open-ended interviews provided a basis for studying the process over time in a few selected cases.

Special techniques and procedures must be used to get this type of personal document. The first problem was to choose the subjects to be interviewed. The decision was based on assessment of the types of information and the quality of information each could provide. One practical consideration involved reaching women who would have the time and would consent to another interview. I also assessed those who could verbalize clearly both their past experiences and their feelings. Next I reflected on the bases to determine whose life histories included some experiences which were substantively and theoretically important. For example: (1) a history of abuse during childhood, (2) a long-term relationship with the man, a relationship in which the pattern of violence had become stabilized, (3) an attempt to leave the man, (4) a possible return to the man, (5) attempts to live on her own, (6) multiple violent relationships. The taped interviews do not represent either typical cases or cases that demonstrate any particular typology. They illustrate how patterns occur within individual cases.

I approached each of three subjects again to explain that I was interested in having them tell their stories in their own words while being tape-recorded. I explained that the material might be used either as a published article or as part of a book. I assured them their names and any details that might identify them would be changed to protect their confidentiality. None of the three women showed any resistance, partly because I had established rapport and some degree of confidence during the earlier interviews.

I also wanted each of the women to review the transcriptions of their interviews to assess if any details were either wrong or too revealing. Only one of the women, Paula, actually did that. I avoided calling Debbie again because any further contact might endanger her. Elizabeth has not let anybody involved in the shelter program know where she is since the taped interview. Pursuing her further would require going to her social worker to get information, and I have chosen not to do that.

Two of the women were interviewed in their homes. The other was interviewed at the place where she was temporarily staying. I had already interviewed these women extensively, so in some cases I asked about specific events, but usually issues emerged with little or no prompting.

To begin the interview, I asked a question. For example: "How did you meet Bill?" When the woman began to talk, I prompted her with further questions to clarify specific points in the interview. In the previous interview these women had indicated specific information which was important to have in the taped interview, for example, a discussion of one particular incident most significant for them. Usually the woman spontaneously mentioned this specific information in the course of talking about her history. However, in some cases I asked her to tell me directly about a specific incident. Just mentioning an incident prompted the woman to talk about that issue.

During the interviews I listened for areas that should be probed further. I took a nonevaluative stance toward what they repeated. In addition, I attempted to assure them of my concern and of the importance of details.

DATA ANALYSIS

Data from the battered women in this sample were analyzed using both quantitative and qualitative methods.

Analysis of Structured Interviews

Chapter 3 presents a description of the demographic and social characteristics of these women, as well as quantitative comparisons of levels of violence and key aspects of the history of violence. The Conflict Tactics Scales provide information on the incidence and frequency of violence acts at time 1 (the year preceding their stay at the shelter) and time 2 (the six months after their stay). The scales are acceptable to respondents, reliable, and seem to have both concurrent and construct validity (Straus, 1979a). Scoring is done in two ways. The first is to count the number of cases that report any act regardless of the frequency category. This provides the incidence for each of the eight violent acts. A Violence Index can be computed by scanning all items K to R to get the percentage of respondents reporting one or more acts of physical violence, and an Abuse Index can be computed by scanning all items N to R to get the percentage of respondents reporting one or more acts serious enough to cause physical harm.

The second scoring technique computes the mean frequency of occurrence for each item. These scores can be combined to get a mean frequency score for the Violence Index (items K to R) and for the Abuse Index (items N to R). Mean frequencies are computed on those actually engaged in each act, omitting those with zero scores.

Chapter 3 also compares changes in the sequence of events surrounding three incidents of violence. The sequence of interaction reported on these incidents sheds some light on the level of simple feedback. Analysis of sequences of events across three incidents provides an indication of how the cybernetic control processes lead to change over time.

Analysis of Taped Interviews

Qualitative material can be analyzed in two basic ways. The first is to code the data according to themes or hypotheses, the second is to present the data in the form of life histories, or what many qualitative researchers call a person's "career." "The concept of career refers to the sequence of occupational and non-occupational positions a person fills through his or her life and the changing definitions of self and the world he or she holds at various stages of that sequence" (Bogdan & Taylor, 1975, p. 121). The present research is not primarily concerned with occupational position. In this case, the concept of "career" is borrowed. This research focuses on the career of a battered wife and on changes over time in definitions both of the self and of the battering. In addition, this approach can bring out changes in social interaction patterns both inside and outside the family.

I chose this latter approach to present the qualitative material. This approach allows the processes that have governed the person's life to emerge from her account. These life histories provide a post hoc interpretation of the sequence of events and the rules that governed the system during previous time periods.

Compared to the ideal of being able to observe patterns emerge over time, post hoc interpretations through life histories are problematic. However, in the case where observation of the total system is impossible, life histories become an alternative source of data on processes that are difficult to study but important to understand.

When these life histories were recorded, the questions asked and the probes used directed attention to the actual sequence of events that occurred. For example, what was the context of the behavior, what sequence of events led to new input into the system, what were the responses of other members of the system to new input, and in turn what further responses followed.

These life histories focus on interaction. They provide a unique source of data on how battering patterns evolve over time by indicating what can happen under specific circumstances in individual cases.

No attempt was made in this research to see how well these life histories fit any prespecified set of hypotheses. In contrast, they are included to provide illustration of wife-battering processes over time.

These life histories were included to help illustrate the temporal/logical hierarchy of stages that appears in Chapter 7. Therefore, it is important to understand how that stage model was developed.

The temporal/logical hierarchy of stages of wife battering and the flow chart of wife-battering processes result from a synthesis of both quantitative and qualitative data. This synthesis is the product of a long process of categorization and conceptual refinement.

The initial interviews included a series of questions about the interaction and particular sequences of events. These specific questions elicited more information about the complexities of the process than could be captured with the prespecified question. Therefore, I recorded verbatim whatever women said when we talked about these sequences of events.

After a third of the initial interviews were completed, I developed an outline of temporal categories dividing the history of the wife-battering career into conceptual units. These roughly corresponded to the stages in the six-stage model that appears in Chapter 7.

Next, records of specific information from individual cases were recorded on charts for different time periods. This specific information included responses to questions directly asked in the first interviews and all spontaneous comments or quotations related to the interaction within the system.

I developed this process of recording and storing data after several interviews, because it was at this point that I realized the interview forms could not capture the complexity of the processes.

From then on, I recorded notes on each interview of events during the several time periods. The initial outline of time periods was modified on the basis of additional information over time. In addition, for each time period I studied the different accounts of interaction for differences and similarities.

Over the year during which data were collected this outline of time periods developed into a model of a temporal/logical hierarchy which is similar to an ideal type model. The description of the model focuses on a typical sequence of events, and is based on a synthesis of all cases. Within each temporal/logical category there is variation. The discussion of the model includes record of variation as well as what was the typical pattern.

Because this is largely exploratory research, no attempt was made to prove this model by reference to either specific cases or any other set of cases. The model emerged over time as a result of a process of conceptual refinement.

At all times during the research, a systems theory approach guided the development of ideas. The questions which prompted the research demanded a focus on processes over time. Systems theory provided the tools to conceptualize processes related to change over time.

The model that developed over time analyzes specific and individual events in the life histories of battered women with the abstract concepts of a systems approach. The description of the processes within the time sequences shifted frequently from the particular to the very abstract. This model synthesizes and punctuates the process for analytical purposes.

To illustrate the entire process within individual cases, I decided it was necessary to include the life histories of several individual women. These illustrative cases are presented with as little editing as possible. The questions that elicited the life history are also included. The inclusion of these complete life histories is based on two premises. The first is that the individual cases can illustrate some of the processes that have been abstractly analyzed in the model developed to represent the total process over time. The second premise is that understanding the woman's perspective on the wife-battering process is necessary for a complete understanding.

The methodological limitations of this study are obvious. Data from all members of the family system, and observation over time of the entire process would have provided a more complete basis for a systems theory of the wife-battering process. Given the impracticality of those alternatives, the research presented here does indicate how processes of change occur over time. At this stage in the development of systems theory within the family area, it is an important step to be finally asking systems questions. In future research I hope these questions will be explored further.

First Interview

code # _____

First, I'd like to ask you some general questions about yourself and other family members.

1. Your age on your last birthday _____
2. Your partner's age on his last birthday _____
3. Marital status
   1. single
   2. married
   3. living with partner of opposite sex
   4. separated
   5. divorced
   6. widowed
4. How long have you been married or living together?
   _____ years _____ months
5. Have you been married or lived with someone else before?
   _____ yes _____ no
6. How long did that relationship last?
   _____ years _____ months
7. If so, how did that relationship end?
   1. separation
   2. divorce
   3. death
   4. desertion
   5. other _____
8. Were there any children from this relationship?
   _____ yes _____ no # _____
9. Tell me the ages of these children. Do they live with you?

age	live with you (yes or no)
_____	_____
_____	_____
_____	_____

10. Has your partner/husband been married or lived with someone else before?

_____ yes _____ no

11. If so how long did that relationship last?

_____ years _____ months

12. If so how did that relationship end?
    1. separation
    2. divorce
    3. death
    4. desertion
    5. other _____

13. Were there any children from this relationship?

_____ yes _____ no # _____

14. What are the ages of these children? Do they live with you?

age	live with you (yes or no)
_____	_____
_____	_____
_____	_____

15. Do you and your present partner/husband have any children of your own?
    1. yes
    2. no

16. What are their ages? Do they live with you?

age	live with you (yes or no)
_____	_____
_____	_____
_____	_____
_____	_____

17. What is your religious preference?
    1. Roman Catholic
    2. Eastern Orthodox
    3. Protestant
    4. Jewish
    5. none
    6. other _____

18. What is the highest grade or year you completed in school?

	RESPONDENT	PARTNER/HUSBAND
some grade school	1	1
completed grade school (8th grade)	2	2
some high school	3	3
completed high school	4	4
completed high school and also had other training but not college	5	5
some college	6	6

completed college	7	7
some graduate work	8	8
graduate degree	9	9
don't know	x	x

19. How about your partner/husband? What is the highest grade or year he completed?

20. What is the predominant ethnic background of yourself and your partner?

	RESPONDENT	PARTNER/HUSBAND
Indian	1	1
Irish	2	2
Italian	3	3
French-Canadian	4	4
Eastern European	5	5
Greek	6	6
Black	7	7
Spanish	8	8
English	9	9
American	10	10
other _____	11	11
don't know	x	x

21. Are you presently employed?
    1. full-time
    2. part-time
    3. student
    4. unemployed, looking for a job
    5. housewife
    6. unemployed, not looking for a job
    7. disabled
    8. retired

22. What is your occupation or job title? _____

_____

23. What do you do at this job? _____

_____

24. How long have you worked at this job? _____

25. Did you work before this job?
    1. yes
    2. no

26. At what point in your marital relationship did you work?
    1. at the beginning, but not after children
    2. not when children were under 3 years
    3. not when children were under 6 years
    4. not when children were under 12 years
    5. not when children were living at home
    6. not at all in the marriage

    7. during the entire marriage

    8. other EXPLAIN _____

27. Taking all things together, how do you feel about your work?
    1. very unsatisfied
    2. unsatisfied
    3. satisfied
    4. very satisfied

28. How satisfied are you with your earnings?
    1. very unsatisfied
    2. unsatisfied
    3. satisfied
    4. very satisfied

29. Taking all things together, how did your partner feel about your work when you first began?
    1. very unsatisfied
    2. unsatisfied
    3. satisfied
    4. very satisfied

30. How does your partner feel about your work now?
    1. very unsatisfied
    2. unsatisfied
    3. satisfied
    4. very satisfied

31. Can you think of any changes in your relationship with your partner that came about as a result of your working, or at approximately the same time as your working—such as decreased time together, more pressure due to household demands plus work demands, increase in sharing of work related concerns, increased enjoyment of leisure due to increased income, decrease in economic strain due to increased income?

_____

_____

_____

32. Is your partner/husband currently employed?
    1. full-time
    2. part-time
    3. student
    4. unemployed, looking for a job
    5. househusband
    6. unemployed, not looking for a job
    7. disabled
    8. retired
    9. other EXPLAIN _____

33. What is his occupation or job title? _____

_____

34. What does he do at this job? _____

_____

35. How long has he worked at this job? _____

36. Were there any times during your marital relationship that he was not
    employed?
    1. once
    2. a few times
    3. several times
    4. many times

37. Taking all things together, how do you think he feels about his work?
    1. very unsatisfied
    2. unsatisfied
    3. satisfied
    4. very satisfied

38. How satisfied do you think he is with his earnings?
    1. very unsatisfied
    2. unsatisfied
    3. satisfied
    4. very satisfied

39. How satisfied are you with your partner's earnings?
    1. very unsatisfied
    2. unsatisfied
    3. satisfied
    4. very satisfied

40. Which of the following groups comes closest to your income and your
    partner's income in the last year?

	RESPONDENT	PARTNER/HUSBAND
none	1	1
less than $1000	2	2
$1000 to $2499	3	3
$2500 to $3999	4	4
$4000 to $5999	5	5
$6000 to $7999	6	6
$8000 to $9999	7	7
$10,000 to $11,999	8	8
$12,000 to $14,999	9	9
$15,000 to $19,999	10	10
$20,000 to $24,999	11	11
$25,000 to $29,999	12	12
$30,000 to $34,999	13	13
$35,000 and over	14	14
don't know	x	x
sources other than work _____		

41. Do you:
    1. own your own home
    2. rent a house
    3. rent an apartment
    4. live with relatives
    5. live with friends
42. Where did you live before you were married or lived with partner?
    1. with parents
    2. with other relatives
    3. with friends
    4. own house or apartment
    5. other _____
43. What did you do before you were married?
    1. worked part-time
    2. worked full-time
    3. student
    4. did not work
    5. other _____
44. If you were married or lived with someone before, how long a time was there between relationships?
    _____ years _____ months
45. What did you do during this time?
    1. worked part-time
    2. worked full-time
    3. student
    4. did not work
    5. other _____
46. Where did you live during this time?
    1. with parents
    2. with other relatives
    3. with friends
    4. own house or apartment
    5. other _____
47. Did you live with your mother and father all the time you were growing up?
    1. yes
    2. no EXPLAIN (Was there any abuse in this situation?) _____
    _____
    _____
48. Did your partner/husband live with his parents all the time he was growing up?
    1. yes
    2. no EXPLAIN (Was there any abuse in this situation?) _____
    _____
    _____

49. Do any of your parents or in-laws live with you?
    1. yes EXPLAIN _____
    2. no
50. How far away from you do they live (approximate miles)? (answer in chart below)
51. How often do you see them? (answer in chart below)
    1. every day
    2. twice a week
    3. once a week
    4. twice a month
    5. once a month
    6. a few times a year
    7. once a year or less
52. What is their marital status? (answer in chart below)
    1. single
    2. married
    3. living with partner of opposite sex
    4. separated
    5. divorced
    6. widowed
    7. deceased

Chart for questions 50, 51, and 52

	50	51	52
mother			
father			
mother-in-law			
father-in-law			

ANY SPECIAL CIRCUMSTANCES _____

_____
_____
_____

53. During the time you were growing up, how much does each of these statements describe your mother's and your father's treatment of you?

	MOTHER	FATHER
a. I could talk with him/ her about everything	0 1 2 3 4	0 1 2 3 4
b. Comforted me and helped me when I had troubles	0 1 2 3 4	0 1 2 3 4
c. Taught me things which I wanted to learn	0 1 2 3	0 1 2 3 4
d. Helped me with things when I didn't understand	0 1 2 3 4	0 1 2 3 4
e. When punishing me, explained why	0 1 2 3 4	0 1 2 3 4

  f. Demanded that I believe

    as they wanted me to   0 1 2 3 4 0 1 2 3 4

  g. Scolded and yelled at me   0 1 2 3 4 0 1 2 3 4

  h. Hit or slapped me   0 1 2 3 4 0 1 2 3 4

  0—never 1—sometimes 2—frequently 3—usually 4—always or almost always

54. When you last lived with your mother, how close did you feel to her?

  1. very close

  2. close

  3. somewhat close

  4. not close

  5. distant

55. When you last lived with your father, how close did you feel to him?

  1. very close

  2. close

  3. somewhat close

  4. not close

  5. distant

56. Do you have anyone you can talk to when you have problems or are feeling low or depressed?

  1. yes

  2. no

57. Is this person:

  1. partner/husband

  2. one of your children

  3. mother

  4. father

  5. mother-in-law

  6. father-in-law

  7. other family member; who? _____

  8. close friend

  9. clergy

  10. social worker

  11. doctor

  12. counselor

  13. other _____

58. How long have you and this person been close?

  1. all my life

  2. several years

  3. about a year

  4. several months

  5. several weeks

  6. a very short time

59. How important is this relationship to you?

  1. not very important

2. somewhat important
3. important
4. very important

60. Does your partner/husband have anyone he can talk to when he has problems or is feeling low or depressed?
    1. yes
    2. no
    3. don't know

61. Is this person:
    1. respondent
    2. one of his children
    3. mother
    4. father
    5. mother-in-law
    6. father-in-law
    7. other family member; who? _____
    8. close friend
    9. clergy
    10. social worker
    11. doctor
    12. counselor
    13. other _____

62. How long have he and this person been close?
    1. all his life
    2. several years
    3. about a year
    4. several months
    5. several weeks
    6. a very short time

63. How important do you think this relationship is to him?
    1. not very important
    2. somewhat important
    3. important
    4. very important

64. How often can you discuss personal things that bother you with your partner?
    1. never
    2. sometimes
    3. half the time
    4. usually
    5. always

65. How important is it to you to be able to discuss things that bother you with your partner/husband?
    1. not very important
    2. somewhat important

    3. important

    4. very important

66. If you and your husband were separated, who do you think would lose the most?

    a. emotionally

        1. husband

        2. wife

        3. both the same

    b. financially

        1. husband

        2. wife

        3. both the same

67. If you and your husband separated who would be able to most easily replace the relationship?

    a. emotionally

        1. husband

        2. wife

        3. both the same

    b. financially

        1. husband

        2. wife

        3. both the same

68. How difficult would it be for you to find new sources of emotional involvement?

    1. impossible

    2. very difficult

    3. somewhat difficult

    4. not very difficult

    5. easy

69. How difficult would it be for you to find new sources of financial support?

    1. impossible

    2. very difficult

    3. somewhat difficult

    4. not very difficult

    5. easy

70. During the past year how would you describe the degree of happiness of your marriage?

    1. very unhappy

    2. unhappy

    3. not too happy

    4. just about average

    5. a little happier than average

    6. very happy

7. extremely happy

71. What would you like to have happen in your relationship with your partner?
    1. reconciled as it has been during the past year
    2. reconciled on new terms
    3. separate
    4. divorce
    5. other _____

72. What do you think is most likely to happen in your relationship taking all things into consideration?
    1. reconciled as it has been during the past year
    2. reconciled on new terms
    3. separate
    4. divorce
    5. other _____

73. Why do you think this will happen? _____
    _____
    _____

74. I would like to ask how similar or different you and your partner are in three things:

    What about being warm and affectionate? Who is more like that, you or your partner/husband?
    1. respondent is more like this
    2. both the same
    3. partner is more like this
    x. don't know

75. What about "smart and intelligent"? Who is more like that?
    1. respondent is more like this
    2. both the same
    3. partner is more like this
    x. don't know

76. And the last one—being "physically attractive"?
    1. respondent is more like this
    2. both the same
    3. partner is more like this
    x. don't know

77. Overall, who do you think has the most say in important decisions in your household—that is, who actually has the most responsibility for making decisions, or the most influence about what decisions are made?
    1. husband always
    2. husband more than wife
    3. husband and wife exactly the same
    4. wife more than husband
    5. wife always

78. Parents and children use many different ways of trying to settle differences between them. I'm going to read a list of things you and [child] might have done when you had a dispute. I would like you to tell me how often you did it with [child] in the last year.

	RESPONDENT								EVER HAPPENED			PARTNER							
	never	once	twice	3–5 times	6–10 times	11–20 times	more than 20 times	don't know	yes	no	don't know	never	once	twice	3–5 times	6–10 times	11–20 times	more than 20 times	don't know
a. Discussed the issue calmly	0	1	2	3	4	5	6	x	1	2	x	0	1	2	3	4	5	6	x
b. Got information to back up your/his or her side of things	0	1	2	3	4	5	6	x	1	2	x	0	1	2	3	4	5	6	x
c. Brought in or tried to bring in someone to help settle things	0	1	2	3	4	5	6	x	1	2	x	0	1	2	3	4	5	6	x
d. Insulted or swore at the other one	0	1	2	3	4	5	6	x	1	2	x	0	1	2	3	4	5	6	x
e. Sulked and/or refused to talk about it	0	1	2	3	4	5	6	x	1	2	x	0	1	2	3	4	5	6	x
f. Stomped out of the room or house (or yard)	0	1	2	3	4	5	6	x	1	2	x	0	1	2	3	4	5	6	x
g. Cried	0	1	2	3	4	5	6	x	1	2	x	0	1	2	3	4	5	6	x
h. Did or said something to spite the other one	0	1	2	3	4	5	6	x	1	2	x	0	1	2	3	4	5	6	x
i. Threatened to hit or throw something at the other one	0	1	2	3	4	5	6	x	1	2	x	0	1	2	3	4	5	6	x
j. Threw or smashed or hit or kicked something	0	1	2	3	4	5	6	x	1	2	x	0	1	2	3	4	5	6	x
k. Threw something at other one	0	1	2	3	4	5	6	x	1	2	x	0	1	2	3	4	5	6	x
l. Pushed, grabbed, or shoved the other one	0	1	2	3	4	5	6	x	1	2	x	0	1	2	3	4	5	6	x

	never	once	twice	3–5 times	6–10 times	11–20 times	more than 20 times	don't know		never	once	twice	3–5 times	6–10 times	11–20 times	more than 20 times	don't know				
m. Slapped or spanked the other one	0	1	2	3	4	5	6	x		1	2	x		0	1	2	3	4	5	6	x
n. Kicked, bit, or hit with fist	0	1	2	3	4	5	6	x		1	2	x		0	1	2	3	4	5	6	x
o. Hit or tried to hit with something	0	1	2	3	4	5	6	x		1	2	x		0	1	2	3	4	5	6	x
p. Beat up the other one	0	1	2	3	4	5	6	x		1	2	x		0	1	2	3	4	5	6	x
q. Threatened with a knife or gun	0	1	2	3	4	5	6	x		1	2	x		0	1	2	3	4	5	6	x
r. Used a knife or gun	0	1	2	3	4	5	6	x		1	2	x		0	1	2	3	4	5	6	x
s. Other (PROBE) _____	0	1	2	3	4	5	6	x		1	2	x		0	1	2	3	4	5	6	x

79. When you and [child] have had a disagreement, have you *ever* [ITEM]?

80. Now, I would like you to tell me how often your partner did each thing with the child or children.

81. No matter how well a couple gets along, there are times when they disagree on major decisions, get annoyed about something the other person does, or just have spats or fights because they're in a bad mood or tired or for some other reason. They also use many different ways of trying to settle their differences. I'm going to read a list of some things that you and your partner might have done when you had a dispute, and would first like you to tell me how often you did it in the past year.

	RESPONDENT IN PAST YEAR									PARTNER IN PAST YEAR									EVER HAPPENED		
	never	once	twice	3–5 times	6–10 times	11–20 times	more than 20 times	don't know		never	once	twice	3–5 times	6–10 times	11–20 times	more than 20 times	don't know		yes	no	don't know
a. Discussed the issue calmly	0	1	2	3	4	5	6	x		0	1	2	3	4	5	6	x		1	2	x
b. Got information to back up your/his side of things	0	1	2	3	4	5	6	x		0	1	2	3	4	5	6	x		1	2	x
c. Brought in or tried to bring in someone to help settle things	0	1	2	3	4	5	6	x		0	1	2	3	4	5	6	x		1	2	x
d. Insulted or swore at the other one	0	1	2	3	4	5	6	x		0	1	2	3	4	5	6	x		1	2	x

	RESPONDENT IN PAST YEAR								PARTNER IN PAST YEAR								EVER HAPPENED		
	never	once	twice	3–5 times	6–10 times	11–20 times	more than 20 times	don't know	never	once	twice	3–5 times	6–10 times	11–20 times	more than 20 times	don't know	yes	no	don't know
e. Sulked and/or refused to talk about it	0	1	2	3	4	5	6	x	0	1	2	3	4	5	6	x	1	2	x
f. Stomped out of the room or house (or yard)	0	1	2	3	4	5	6	x	0	1	2	3	4	5	6	x	1	2	x
g. Cried	0	1	2	3	4	5	6	x	0	1	2	3	4	5	6	x	1	2	x
h. Did or said something to spite the other one	0	1	2	3	4	5	6	x	0	1	2	3	4	5	6	x	1	2	x
i. Threatened to hit or throw something at the other one	0	1	2	3	4	5	6	x	0	1	2	3	4	5	6	x	1	2	x
j. Threw or smashed or hit or kicked something	0	1	2	3	4	5	6	x	0	1	2	3	4	5	6	x	1	2	x
k. Threw something at other one	0	1	2	3	4	5	6	x	0	1	2	3	4	5	6	x	1	2	x
l. Pushed, grabbed, or shoved the other one	0	1	2	3	4	5	6	x	0	1	2	3	4	5	6	x	1	2	x
m. Slapped the other one	0	1	2	3	4	5	6	x	0	1	2	3	4	5	6	x	1	2	x
n. Kicked, bit, or hit with fist	0	1	2	3	4	5	6	x	0	1	2	3	4	5	6	x	1	2	x
o. Hit or tried to hit with something	0	1	2	3	4	5	6	x	0	1	2	3	4	5	6	x	1	2	x
p. Beat up the other one	0	1	2	3	4	5	6	x	0	1	2	3	4	5	6	x	1	2	x
q. Threatened with a knife or gun	0	1	2	3	4	5	6	x	0	1	2	3	4	5	6	x	1	2	x
r. Used a knife or gun	0	1	2	3	4	5	6	x	0	1	2	3	4	5	6	x	1	2	x
s. Other (PROBE) _____	0	1	2	3	4	5	6	x	0	1	2	3	4	5	6	x	1	2	x

82. And what about your husband/partner? Tell me how often he [ITEM] in the past year?

83. (For items circled "never" or "don't know" for BOTH people) Did you or your partner/husband ever [ITEM]?

84. I am going to read a list of things that couples do not always agree on. First, I would like you to tell me if this has ever been a problem, and then rank order those items that have been a problem, giving 1 to the problem that has been of most concern, etc., until you get to 3.

	EVER A PROBLEM (yes or no)	RANK (1 = high, etc.)
a. arguments over money	_____	_____
b. husband jealous over wife's involvements	_____	_____
c. wife jealous over husband's involvements	_____	_____
d. husband's use of alcohol or other drugs	_____	_____
e. things about the children	_____	_____
f. sex and expressions of affection	_____	_____
g. household tasks	_____	_____
h. pregnancy or birth control	_____	_____
i. wife's use of alcohol or other drugs	_____	_____
j. husband's income or employment situation	_____	_____
k. wife's income or employment situation	_____	_____
l. other (specify) _____	_____	_____

85. Every couple has its ups and downs, and surveys have shown most people wonder at some time or other whether they should continue their marriage/relationship. What about in your case? Have you ever thought about this?
    1. yes
    2. no
86. If you have, how much have you thought about it?
    1. once
    2. a few times
    3. a lot
87. When you thought about it, did you ever actually separate?
    1. yes
    2. no
    CIRCUMSTANCES _____

    _____
    _____

Now, I would like to talk specifically about the history of violence in your relationship with your partner.

Recall if you can the very first time in your relationship that there was any violence.

88. When was that?
    day _____ month _____ year _____
89. Were you:
    1. married at the time
    2. living together
    3. neither
90. What actually happened during the incident? _____
    _____
    _____
    _____

91. Were there any important events that happened to anyone in the family immediately preceding the incident such as:
    a. loss of job of husband
    b. loss of job of wife
    c. new job of husband
    d. new job of wife
    e. birth of a child
    f. discovery of a pregnancy
    g. death in the family
    h. illness in the family or injury
    i. move to a different house or apartment
    j. move to a different town
    k. complaints by wife
    l. complaints by husband
    m. husband made or lost a good friend
    n. wife made or lost a good friend
    o. problems with extended family members
    p. problems with children
    q. other _____
92. At the immediate time that it happened, were you:
    1. not at all upset
    2. slightly upset
    3. quite upset
    4. very upset
93. Did you feel guilty about what had happened?
    1. yes
    2. no
94. Did you feel angry at yourself?
    1. yes
    2. no
95. Were you angry at your husband?
    1. yes
    2. no
96. Were you angry at other things or people?
    1. yes

2. no

97. Were you willing to "forgive and forget"?

    1. yes
    2. no

98. Who or what do you think was responsible for this incident? _____

_____

_____

    (Attribution) 1. internal to respondent
                   2. internal to partner
                   3. internal to relationship
                   4. external to respondent
                   5. external to partner
                   6. external to relationship

99. The very first time, did you think the incident was:

    1. a normal reaction
    2. good
    3. necessary
    4. bad
    5. didn't think much about it

    EXPLAIN _____

_____

100. What impact did the incident have on you at that time? _____

_____

101. What impact do you think it had on the children? _____

_____

102. What impact do you think it had on your relationship with your partner?

_____

103. At the time that this happened, did you think that this was:

    1. an isolated incident that probably wouldn't happen again
    2. part of a pattern of violence

104. What happened immediately after the incident?

    a. partner left the house
    b. respondent left the house
    c. partner asked forgiveness
    d. respondent asked forgiveness
    e. partner became more violent
    f. respondent became more violent
    g. police called
    h. partner sought help or support from other sources
    i. respondent sought help or support from other sources
    j. someone outside family intervened
    k. someone inside family intervened
    l. return to normal routine
    m. other _____

105. If someone's help was sought after this incident, tell me what happened—that is, whom did you ask for help, and what did he/she do about the problem?

_____

_____

_____

_____

_____

_____

_____

_____

_____

Now, I would like to talk specifically about the incident that happened just before you came here.

106. When did that happen?
     day _____ month _____ year _____

107. Were you:
     1. married at the time
     2. living together
     3. neither

108. What actually happened during the incident? _____

_____

_____

_____

109. Were there any important events that happened to anyone in the family immediately preceding the incident such as:
     a. loss of job of husband
     b. loss of job of wife
     c. new job of husband
     d. new job of wife
     e. birth of a child
     f. discovery of a pregnancy
     g. death in the family
     h. illness in the family or injury
     i. move to a different house or apartment
     j. move to a different town
     k. complaints by wife
     l. complaints by husband
     m. husband made or lost a good friend
     n. wife made or lost a good friend
     o. problems with extended family members
     p. problems with children
     q. other _____

110. At the immediate time that it happened, were you:
    1. not at all upset
    2. slightly upset
    3. quite upset
    4. very upset
111. Did you feel guilty about what had happened?
    1. yes
    2. no
112. Did you feel angry at yourself?
    1. yes
    2. no
113. Were you angry at your husband?
    1. yes
    2. no
114. Were you angry at other things or people?
    1. yes
    2. no
115. Were you willing to "forgive and forget"?
    1. yes
    2. no
116. Who or what do you think was responsible for this incident? _____

    _____

    (Attribution) 1. internal to respondent
                  2. internal to partner
                  3. internal to relationship
                  4. external to respondent
                  5. external to partner
                  6. external to relationship
117. This time, did you think the incident was:
    1. a normal reaction
    2. good
    3. necessary
    4. bad
    5. didn't think much about it
    EXPLAIN _____

    _____

118. What impact did this most recent incident have on you?

    _____

119. What impact do you think this incident had on the children? _____

    _____

120. What impact do you think it had on your relationship with your partner?

    _____

    _____

121. At the time that this happened, did you think that this was:
     1. an isolated incident that probably wouldn't happen again
     2. part of a pattern of violence
122. What happened immediately after the incident?
     a. partner left the house
     b. respondent left the house
     c. partner asked forgiveness
     d. respondent asked forgiveness
     e. partner became more violent
     f. respondent became more violent
     g. police called
     h. partner sought help or support from other sources
     i. respondent sought help or support from other sources
     j. someone outside family intervened
     k. someone inside family intervened
     l. return to normal routine
     m. other _____
123. If someone's help was sought after this incident, tell me what happened—
     that is, whom did you ask for help, and what did he/she do about the
     problem?

     _____
     _____
     _____
     _____
     _____
     _____
     _____
     _____

Now I would like to talk about one other incident between those two we just
talked about that sticks out in your mind as being important.

124. When did that happen?
     day _____ month _____ year _____
125. Were you:
     1. married at the time
     2. living together
     3. neither
126. What actually happened during the incident? _____
     _____
     _____

127. Were there any important events that happened to anyone in the family
     immediately preceding the incident such as:
     a. loss of job of husband

    d. loss of job of wife

    c. new job of husband

    d. new job of wife

    e. birth of a child

    f. discovery of a pregnancy

    g. death in the family

    h. illness in the family or injury

    i. move to a different house or apartment

    j. move to a different town

    k. complaints by wife

    l. complaints by husband

    m. husband made or lost a good friend

    n. wife made or lost a good friend

    o. problems with extended family members

    p. problems with children

    q. other _____

128. At the immediate time that it happened, were you:

    1. not at all upset

    2. slightly upset

    3. quite upset

    4. very upset

129. Did you feel guilty about what had happened?

    1. yes

    2. no

130. Did you feel angry at yourself?

    1. yes

    2. no

131. Were you angry at your husband?

    1. yes

    2. no

132. Were you angry at other things or people?

    1. yes

    2. no

133. Were you willing to "forgive and forget"?

    1. yes

    2. no

134. Who or what do you think was responsible for this incident? _____

_____

_____

    (Attribution) 1. internal to respondent

                 2. internal to partner

                 3. internal to relationship

                 4. external to respondent

                 5. external to partner

                 6. external to relationship

135. This time, did you think the incident was:
     1. a normal reaction
     2. good
     3. necessary
     4. bad
     5. didn't think much about it
     EXPLAIN _____

     _____

136. What impact did this incident have on you? _____

     _____

137. What impact do you think this incident had on the children?

     _____

     _____

138. What impact do you think it had on your relationship with your partner?

     _____

     _____

139. At the time that this happened, did you think it was:
     1. an isolated incident that probably wouldn't happen again
     2. part of a pattern of violence
140. What happened immediately after the incident?
     a. partner left the house
     b. respondent left the house
     c. partner asked forgiveness
     d. respondent asked forgiveness
     e. partner became more violent
     f. respondent became more violent
     g. police called
     h. partner sought help or support from other sources
     i. respondent sought help or support from other sources
     j. someone outside family intervened
     k. someone inside family intervened
     l. return to normal routine
     m. other _____
141. If someone's help was sought after this incident, tell me what happened—
     that is, whom did you ask for help, and what did he/she do about the
     problem?

     _____
     _____
     _____
     _____
     _____
     _____
     _____
     _____

Six-Month Follow-Up Interview

code # _____

First I'd like to ask some general questions about your situation since you left the shelter.

1. Where are you living now?
    1. same house or apartment
    2. different house
    3. different apartment
    4. other _____
2. Are you currently living with:
    1. husband previous to coming to shelter
    2. partner previous to coming to shelter
    3. another partner
    4. relatives _____
    5. friends _____
    6. alone with children
    7. alone without children
    8. other _____
3. Marital status
    1. single
    2. married
    3. living with partner of opposite sex
    4. separated
    5. divorced
    6. widowed
4. If you have been separated or divorced since leaving the shelter how long has it been?
    _____ months _____ weeks _____ days
5. How far away from you does your (former) partner live?
    _____ miles

6. How often do you see him?
   1. every day
   2. twice a week
   3. once a week
   4. twice a month
   5. once a month
   6. a few times in past six months
   7. once in past six months
   8. not at all in past six months
7. Does your (former) partner do any of the following?

                                                check if yes
   1. provide financial support   _____
   2. full-time child care   _____
   3. part-time child care   _____
   4. help with transportation   _____
   5. help with household tasks   _____
   6. provide emotional support   _____
   7. other _____   _____
8. Have you sought his help in any of these areas in the past six months?
   1. yes
   2. no
9. What happened when and if you asked for help? _____
   _____

10. Taking all things together, how do you feel about the status of your rela-
    tionship with your (former) partner?
    1. very unsatisfied
    2. unsatisfied
    3. satisfied
    4. very satisfied
11. At the time that you left the shelter what did you want to have happen in
    your relationship with your partner?
    1. reconciled as it had been during the previous years
    2. reconciled on new terms
    3. separated
    4. divorced
    5. other _____
12. What do you want to have happen in your relationship with your partner
    now?
    1. reconciled as it has been during the previous years
    2. reconciled on new terms
    3. separated
    4. divorced
    5. other _____
13. Why do you want this to happen? _____
    _____

14. If you reconciled with your partner, at the time that you did so, how likely did you think it was that it would work out?
  1. very likely
  2. somewhat likely
  3. unlikely
  4. very unlikely
15. How hopeful were you that it would work out?
  1. very hopeful
  2. somewhat hopeful
  3. not very hopeful
  4. didn't think it would work out
16. Did you experience pressure from any of the following to reconcile or not to?

	reconcile	not to
1. extended family	_____	_____
2. friends (mutual)	_____	_____
3. personal friends	_____	_____
4. children	_____	_____
5. church or clergy	_____	_____
6. counselors or therapists	_____	_____
7. shelter personnel	_____	_____
8. societal expectations	_____	_____
9. partner	_____	_____
10. other _____	_____	_____

17. If you did reconcile once and then left again, how did that decision come about? _____

_____

18. Was there any one or most important thing that made you leave again?

_____

19. Was there any one most important thing that made you reconcile? _____
20. If you have gotten back together, how would you describe the degree of happiness in your relationship now?
  1. very unhappy
  2. unhappy
  3. not too happy
  4. just about average
  5. a little happier than average
  6. very happy
  7. extremely happy
21. If you have gotten back together, overall who has the most say in important decisions in your household—that is, who actually has the most responsibility for making decisions, or the most influence about what decisions are made?
  1. husband always
  2. husband more than wife

3. husband and wife exactly the same
4. wife more than husband
5. wife always

22. Are you presently employed or in job training?
    1. full-time employed
    2. part-time employed
    3. student
    4. unemployed, looking for a job
    5. housewife
    6. unemployed, not looking for a job
    7. disabled
    8. retired
    9. job training program _____

23. What is your occupation, job title, or training title? _____
_____

24. What do you do at this job? _____

25. How long have you worked at this job? _____

26. Have you had other jobs or training since you left the shelter? _____

27. Taking all things together, how do you feel about your work?
    1. very unsatisfied
    2. unsatisfied
    3. satisfied
    4. very satisfied

28. How satisfied are you with your earnings?
    1. very unsatisfied
    2. unsatisfied
    3. satisfied
    4. very satisfied

29. Taking all things together, how does your partner feel about your work?
    1. very unsatisfied
    2. unsatisfied
    3. satisfied
    4. very satisfied
    5. not applicable because not involved with previous partner

30. Is your former partner currently employed?
    1. full-time
    2. part-time
    3. student
    4. unemployed, looking for a job
    5. househusband
    6. unemployed, not looking for a job
    7. disabled
    8. retired

31. What is his occupation or job title? _____

32. What does he do at this job? _____

33. How long has he worked at this job? _____

34. Was there any times during the past six months that he was not employed?
    1. once
    2. twice or more
    3. not employed at all
    4. none

35. Taking all things together, how do you think he feels about his work?
    1. very unsatisfied
    2. unsatisfied
    3. satisfied
    4. very satisfied
    5. don't know

36. How satisfied do you think he is with his earnings?
    1. very unsatisfied
    2. unsatisfied
    3. satisfied
    4. very satisfied
    5. don't know

37. How satisfied are you with your partner's earnings?
    1. very unsatisfied
    2. unsatisfied
    3. satisfied
    4. very satisfied
    5. doesn't apply

38. Which of the following groups comes closest to your income and your (former) partner's income in the last six months?

	RESPONDENT	PARTNER/HUSBAND
none	1	1
less than $1000	2	2
$1000 to $2499	3	3
$2500 to $3999	4	4
$4000 to $5999	5	5
$6000 to $7999	6	6
$8000 to $9999	7	7
$10,000 to $11,999	8	8
$12,000 to $14,999	9	9
$15,000 to $19,999	10	10
$20,000 to $24,999	11	11
$25,000 to $29,999	12	12
$30,000 to $34,999	13	13
$35,000 and over	14	14
don't know	x	x
sources other than work _____		

39. Are your children:
    1. living with you and your partner
    2. living with you alone
    3. living with father
    4. living with other relative
    5. in other living situations
    EXPLAIN _____

40. How difficult has it been for you with the children in the past six months?
    1. impossible
    2. very difficult
    3. somewhat difficult
    4. not very difficult
    5. easy
41. How difficult has it been for you financially in the past six months?
    1. impossible
    2. very difficult
    3. somewhat difficult
    4. not very difficult
    5. easy
42. In the past six months, have you had contact with any of the following people or groups? (answer in chart below)
    1. yes
    2. no
43. How often do you see each of the following? (answer in chart below)
    1. every day
    2. twice a week
    3. once a week
    4. twice a month
    5. once a month
    6. a few times in six months
    7. once in six months
    8. not at all in six months
44. How important is each of these to you? (answer in chart below)
    1. very important
    2. important
    3. slightly important
    4. not at all important

Chart for questions 42, 43, and 44

	42	43	44
extended family	_____	_____	_____
close friends	_____	_____	_____
people at work	_____	_____	_____

a counselor   _____ _____ _____
support group   _____ _____ _____
former residents of shelter   _____ _____ _____
shelter staff   _____ _____ _____
church groups   _____ _____ _____
AA, Al-Anon, or other
  alcoholism services   _____ _____ _____
men friends or dates   _____ _____ _____
men partners in relationships _____ _____ _____
other groups or organizations _____ _____ _____
other people or activities   _____ _____ _____

45. If you have gotten involved in a new relationship with a partner, how long
    has it been?
    _____ months _____ weeks _____ days

46. If you have a new relationship, have you also been involved with or lived
    with anyone else since leaving the shelter?
    EXPLAIN _____
    _____

47. How difficult has it been for you to find new sources of emotional in-
    volvement?
    1. impossible
    2. very difficult
    3. somewhat difficult
    4. not very difficult
    5. easy

48. What are you looking for in a new relationship? _____
    _____
    _____

49. Why is this important? _____
    _____

50. Has there been any violence at all in this relationship? _____
    _____
    _____

References

Allen, C., & Straus, M.A. Resources, power, and husband–wife violence. In M.A. Straus & G. Hotaling (Eds.), *Social causes of husband–wife violence*. Minneapolis, Minn.: University of Minnesota Press, 1979.

Bandura, A. *Aggression—A social learning analysis*. Englewood Cliffs, N.J.: Prentice-Hall, 1973.

Bard, M., & Zacker, J. The prevention of family violence: Dilemma of community intervention. *Journal of Marriage and the Family*, 1971, *33*, 677–682.

Bard, M., & Zacker, J. Assaultiveness and alcohol use in family disputes—Police perceptions. *Criminology*, 1974, *12*, 281–292.

Bateson, G. *Steps to an ecology of mind*. New York: Ballantine Books, 1972.

Becker, H. *Outsiders: Studies in the sociology of deviance*. New York: The Free Press, 1963.

Bell, J. N. Rescuing the battered wife. *Human Behavior*, 1977, June, 16–23.

Berkowitz, L. *Aggression: A social psychological analysis*. New York: McGraw-Hill, 1962.

Blood, R.O., & Wolfe, D.M. *Husbands and wives: The dynamics of married living*. New York: The Free Press, 1960.

Bogdan, R., & Taylor, S.J. *Introduction to qualitative research methods*. New York: John Wiley & Sons, 1975.

Broderick, C.B. Beyond the five conceptual frameworks: A decade of development in family theory. *Journal of Marriage and the Family*, 1971, *33*, 139–159.

Broderick, C.B., & Smith, J. The general systems approach to the family. In W.R. Burr, R. Hill, F. Nye, & I.L. Reiss (Eds.), *Contemporary theories about the family*. New York: The Free Press, 1979.

Buckley, W. *Sociology and modern systems theory*. Englewood Cliffs, N.J.: Prentice-Hall, 1967.

Campbell, D.T., & Fiske, D.W. Convergent and discriminant validation by the multitrait–multimethod matrix. *Psychological Bulletin*, *56*, 81–105.

Campbell, D.T., & Stanley J.C. *Experimental and quasi-experimental designs for research*. Chicago: Rand McNally, 1966.

Caplan, G. Patterns of parental response to the crisis of premature birth: A preliminary approach to modifying mental health outcome. *Psychiatry*, 1960, *23*, 365–374.

Carlson, B.E. Battered women and their assailants. *Social Work*, 1977, *2*(61), 455–460.

Chesler, P. Women as psychiatric and psychotherapeutic patients. *Journal of Marriage and the Family*, 1971, *33*(4), 746–759.

Coleman, D.H., & Straus, M.A. *Alcohol abuse and family violence*. Paper presented at American Sociological Association meetings, August 1979.

Cuber, J., & Harroff, P. *The significant Americans: A study of sexual behavior among the affluent*. New York: Appleton, 1965.

Dobash, R. & Dobash, R.P. Love, honour and obey: Institutional ideologies and the struggle for battered women. *Contemporary Crisis*, 1977, *1*, 403–415.

Dobash, R.E. & Dobash R.P. *With friends like these who needs enemies: Institutional supports for the patriarchy and violence against women.* Paper presented at the IX World Congress of Sociology, Uppsala, Sweden, 1978.

Dollard, J., Doob, L.W., Miller, N.E., Mowrer, O.H. & Sears, R.R. *Frustration and aggression.* New Haven, Conn.: Yale University Press, 1939.

Etzioni, A. Violence. In R.K. Merton & R.A. Nisbet (Eds.), *Contemporary social problems* (3rd ed.). New York: Harcourt Brace Jovanovich, 1971.

Erikson, K.T. *The wayward puritans.* New York: John Wiley & Sons, 1966.

Field, M.H., & Field, H.F. Marital violence and the criminal process: Neither justice nor peace. *Social Service Review*, 1973, *47*, 2.

Fields, M.D. Wife beating: The hidden offense. *New York Law Journal*, 1976, *175*(83), 1–7.

Geen, R.G. *Aggression.* Reprint by General Learning Corporation, Morristown, N.J., 1972.

Gelles, R.J. *The violent home: A study of physical agression between husbands and wives.* Beverly Hills, Calif.: Sage Publications, 1972.

Gelles, R.J. Abused wives: Why do they stay? *Journal of Marriage and the Family.* November, 1976, 659–668.

Gelles, R.J. Violence and pregnancy: A note on the extent of the problem and needed services. *Family Coordinator*, 1977a, *26*, 81–86.

Gelles, R.J. No place to go—The social dynamics of marital violence. In M. Roy (Ed.), *Battered women—A psychosociological study of domestic violence.* New York: Van Nostrand Reinhold, 1977b.

Gelles, R.J., & Straus, M.A. Determinants of violence in the family: Toward a theoretical integration. In W.R. Burr, R. Hill, F.E. Nye, & I.L. Reiss (Eds.), *Contemporary theories about the family.* New York: The Free Press, 1979.

Gelles, R.J. Violence in the family: A review of research in the seventies. *Journal of Marriage and the Family*, 1980, *42*(4), 873–885.

Goffman, E. *Asylums.* Garden City, N.Y.: Doubleday/Anchor Press, 1961.

Goldstein, J.H., Davis, R.W., & Herman, D. Escalation of aggression: Experimental studies. *Journal of Personality and Social Psychology*, 1975, *31*(1), 162–170.

Goode, W. Force and violence in the family. *Journal of Marriage and the Family*, 1971, *33*, 624–636.

Haley, J. *Strategies of psychotherapy.* New York: Grune & Stratton, 1963.

Hill, R. Modern systems theory and the family: A confrontation. *Social Science Information*, 1971, *10*, 7–26.

Hoffman, L. Deviation-amplifying processes in natural groups. In J. Haley (Ed.), *Changing families*, New York: Grune & Stratton, 1971.

Hotaling, G.T. Facilitating violence—why intimates attribute aggression. In M.A. Straus & G. Hotaling (Eds.), *Social causes of husband–wife violence.* Minneapolis, Minn.: University of Minnesota Press, 1979.

Jackson, D. The question of family homeostasis. *Psychiatric Quarterly*, 1957, *31*, 79–90.

Janoff-Bulman, R. *Self-blame in rape victims: Control-maintenance strategy.* Paper presented as part of symposium, New Directions for Control Research, American Psychological Association meeting, Toronto, Canada, 1978.

Kantor, D., & Lehr, W. *Inside the family.* San Francisco: Jossey-Bass, 1975.

LaRossa, R. *Conflict and power in marriage: Expecting the first child.* Beverly Hills, Calif.: Sage Publications, 1977.

LeMasters, E.E. Parenthood as crisis. *Marriage and Family Living*, 1957, *19*, 352–355.

Lemert, E.M. *Human deviance: Social problems and social control.* Englewood Cliffs, N.J.: Prentice-Hall, 1967.

Lewis, O. *Five families.* New York: Basic Books, 1959.

Lowenthal, M.F., & Haven C. Interaction and adaptation: Intimacy as a critical variable. *American Sociological Review,* 1968, *33,* 20–30.

Marcovitch, A. Refuges for battered women. *Social Work Today,* 1976, 7(2), 34–35.

Martin, D. *Battered wives.* San Francisco: Glide, 1976.

Mead, M., & MacGregor, F.C. *Growth and culture: A photographic study of Balinese children.* New York: C.P. Putnam's Sons, 1951.

Megargee, E.I. *The psychology of violence and aggression.* Reprint by General Learning Corporation, Morristown, N.J., 1972.

Miller, N.E. The frustration–aggression hypothesis. *Psychological Review,* 1941, *48,* 337–342. Reprinted in L. Berkowitz (Ed.), *Roots of aggression.* New York: Atherton, 1941.

Nichols, B. The abused wife problem. *Social Casework,* 1976, *57,* 27–32.

O'Brien, J.E. Violence in divorce-prone families. *Journal of Marriage and the Family,* 1971, *33,* 692–698.

Pagelow, M.D. *Battered women—A new perspective.* Unpublished manuscript, University of California, 1977.

Parnas, R. The police response to domestic disturbance. *Wisconsin Law Review,* 1977, *914,* 914–960.

Patterson, G.R., Cobb, J.A., & Ray, R.S. A social engineering technology for retraining families of aggressive boys. In H.E. Adams & I.P. Unikel (Eds.), *Issues and trends in behavior therapy.* Springfield, Ill.: Charles C Thomas, 1972.

Piotrkowski, C.S. *Work and the family system.* New York: The Free Press, 1979.

Raush, H.L., Berry, W.A., Hertel, R.K., & Swain, M.A. Varieties of consensual experience: A theory for relating family interaction to individual thinking. *Family Process,* 1974, *10,* 1–28.

Reiss, D. Varieties of consensual experience: A theory for relating family interaction to individual thinking. *Family Process,* 1971, *10,* 1–28.

Scanzoni, J. *Opportunity in the family.* New York: The Free Press, 1970.

Scheff, T.J. *Being mentally ill.* Chicago: Aldine, 1966.

Scherer, K.R., Abeles, R.P., & Fischer, C.S. *Human aggression and conflict.* Englewood Cliffs, N.J.: Prentice-Hall, 1975.

Scott, P.D. Battered wives. *British Journal of Psychiatry,* 1974, *125*(11), 433.

Shainess, N. Psychological aspects of wifebeating. In M. Roy (Ed.), *Battered women—A psychosociological study of domestic violence.* New York: Van Nostrand Reinhold, 1977.

Snell, J.E., Rosenwald, R.J., & Robey, A. The wifebeater's wife: A study of family interaction. *Archives of General Psychiatry,* 1964, *11,* 107–113.

Speer, D.C. Family systems: Morphogenesis, or is homeostasis enough? *Family Process,* 1970, *9,* 259.

Sprey, J. The family as a system in conflict. *Journal of Marriage and the Family,* 1969, *31,* 699–706.

Sprey, J. On the management of conflict in families. *Journal of Marriage and the Family,* 1971, *33,* 722–731.

Steinmetz, S.K. *Cycle of violence—Assertive, aggressive, and abusive family interaction.* New York: Praeger Publishers, 1977.

Steinmetz, S.K., & Straus, M.A. Family as a cradle of violence. *Society,* 1973, *10*(6), 50–56.

Straus, M.A. A general systems theory approach to a theory of violence between family members. *Social Science Information,* 1973, *12,* 105–125.

Straus, M.A. Leveling, civility and violence in the family. *Journal of Marriage and the Family,* 1974, *36,* 13–29.

Straus, M.A. Sexual inequality, cultural norms, and wife beating. *Victimology,* 1976, *1,* 54–70.

Straus, M.A. Wife beating: How common and why? *Victimology*, 1977a, *2*, 443–458.

Straus, M.A. Sociological perspective on the prevention and treatment of wifebeating. In M. Roy, (Ed.), *Battered women—A psychosociological study of domestic violence.* New York: Van Nostrand Reinhold, 1977b.

Straus, M.A. Measuring intrafamily conflict and violence: The Conflict Tactics (CT) Scales. *Journal of Marriage and the Family*, 1979a, *41*, 75–98.

Straus, M.A. *A sociological perspective on the causes of family violence.* Paper presented at the American Association for the Advancement of Science, Houston, Tex., January 6, 1979b.

Straus, M.A., Gelles, R., & Steinmetz, S.K. *Behind closed doors: Violence in the American family.* Garden City, N.Y.: Doubleday/Anchor Press, 1980.

Tidmarsh, M. Violence in marriage: The relevance of structural factors. *Social Work Today*, 1976, *7*(2), 36–38.

Van Stolk, M. Battered women, battered children. *Children Today*, 1976, March–April, 8–12.

Walker, L.E. Battered women and learned helplessness. *Victimology*, 1977–1978, *2*, 525–534.

Walker, L.E. *The battered woman.* New York: Harper & Row, 1979.

Watzlawick, P., Beavin, J. H., & Jackson, D.D. *Pragmatics of human communication: A study of interaction patterns, pathologies, and paradoxes.* New York: W.W. Norton, 1967.

Yllo, K., & Straus, M.A. Interpersonal violence among married and cohabiting couples. *Family Relations*, 1980, *30*, 339–347.

Index